Our Like Will Not
Be There Again

Mar ná beidh ár leithéidí arís ann.
—Tomás Ó Crohan, *The Islandman*

Our Like Will Not Be There Again

Notes from the West of Ireland

Lawrence Millman

Little, Brown and Company   *Boston   Toronto*

Library of Congress Cataloging in Publication Data

Millman, Lawrence.
   Our like will not be there again.

   1. Storytellers—Ireland.   2. Tales, Irish.
3. Ireland—Social life and customs—20th century.
I. Title.
GR153.5.M54   390'.09417   77-74723
ISBN 0-316-54235-0

FIRST EDITION

T05/77

The author is grateful to Curtis Brown, Ltd., for permission to re-
print four lines from "Down Wanton Down" from *Collected Poems* by
Robert Graves. Copyright © 1939, 1955, 1958, 1961, 1965 by Robert
Graves.

Designed by Christine Benders

*Published simultaneously in Canada
by Little, Brown & Company (Canada) Limited*

PRINTED IN THE UNITED STATES OF AMERICA

Imagination and memory are but one thing, which for divers considerations hath divers names.

— Hobbes, *Leviathan*

If I were asked what man I most envied, I should answer without hesitation: the one who, taking his ease among words, lives there naively, by reflex, neither questioning nor identifying them with signs, as if they corresponded to reality itself.

— E. M. Cioran, *The Temptation to Exist*

Oh hand in hand, let us return to the land of our birth, the bogs, the moors, the glens, the lakes, the rivers, the streams, the brooks, the mists, the — er — fens, the — er — glens, by tonight's mail-train.

— Samuel Beckett, *Murphy*

Preface

Most of the speech in this book is transcribed from conversations I recorded in 1975 in the west of Ireland, "the last place in the world where conversation is not dead," according to one man. I went with my tape recorder to fields, pubs, isolated farmhouses, tinker encampments, doss houses, forges, and country crossroads; and I recorded wonder tales, jokes, violent opinions, and self-contained monologues. These conversations I present here as they happened, with editing kept to a minimum.

Wherever possible, I have tried in my own observations to take account of the viewpoints of the people themselves. They have no spokesmen, other than themselves, who are *speech-men;* and that is part of their dilemma, living by the spoken rather than the written word. An even larger part of it is that, with the current Irish trend away from subsistence agriculture and toward an urban society based on industry, they have become all but superfluous. No words in any form can redeem this loss of importance.

This book is about storytelling. But storytelling has not been my goal. It is rather an image that helps tie the other images together. For with the near-vanishing of the art of storytelling, there has also been a lowering of life, a decline in communal ways. Now, community means the European Economic Community, which the Irish Republic joined in 1973, giving up its hopes for economic independence. Today Europe, tomorrow the world? Unfortunately, once there is a global community, there is no community to speak of, only certain manners duplicated in the Aran Islands and Hawaii, Kerry, and Mali. Such shrunk garments invariably provide discomfort to their wearers.

The story of the west of Ireland will be over when it is no different from any other west.

The people:

Tomás Walsh, Seán Murphy, and Tadhg Sugrue are native Irish speakers, of whom there are perhaps thirty thousand left, living in the outlying areas of Kerry, Connemara, and Donegal. In their talks with me, these men spoke mostly in English; their stories, however, could only be told in Irish, because that was the language in which such stories had always been told. I might add that their ordinary talk is less ungrammatical than it would at first appear to be. Much of it, though in English, consists of idioms taken over from Irish, where they would be perfectly acceptable.

The brogue of the tinkers is reproduced just the way it sounds. In print, it may look a little stagey, rather like the way Irish people always seemed to talk in nineteenth century novels.

But many of these people do, in fact, cling to values and attitudes that are nineteenth century in origin, if not earlier. And they do not read novels.

My greatest debt is to the men and women of the West, who took me in and told me their stories. I have repaid this kindness in the smallest of ways, by changing their names and deliberately blurring the localities where they live. For they are people who prefer anonymity in every respect.

The following people also donated wit and wisdom, bicycles, motorcars, lodgings, or general support: Sister Brigid, of Galway; "Sonny" Canavan, of Listowel; Crochúr Ó Ceileachaer, of Belmullet; Cathrine Crohan, of Springfield, Massachusetts; Mick Cunnane, of Inishbofin; Bobbie Fitz, of Castlegregory; Peter Green, of Athlone; Pats Keane, of Murreigh, west Kerry; John B. Keane, playwright and publican, of Listowel; Tomás Kennedy, of Cloosh, west Kerry; George McGrath, of Tuam; Tim O'Shea, of Dublin; Seán Ó Súilleabháin, of Dublin; the late Ray Phillips; and Tamar Scott, of Galway, who helped with the translation of Seán Murphy's story.

The Great Blasket — York, Maine 1975–1976

Contents

Our Like Will Not
Be There Again

Proem: ... And He Not Far from Quiet Hisself

> "Beyond the Wild Wood comes the Wide World" — said the Rat. "And that's something that doesn't matter, either to you or me. I've never been there, and I'm never going, nor you either. ..."
>
> — Kenneth Grahame, *The Wind in the Willows*

THIS IS NO COUNTRY for young men. It is scarcely a country for any sort of man. It prefers earlier stages of evolution, which change only to become larger versions of themselves. That most tenacious of molluscs, the limpet, grows majestic on its rocks. Ridges of sullen infertility nurture sheep better than they do people. And a ground fit for pasturing cattle refuses most attempts to make it yield human food as well. Gaunt headlands and cliffs echo with the screechings of seabirds; their massed

3

droppings, which adorn rocks with white scatter-patterns, poison the nostrils. On islands, even the most barren of wind-scudded skerries, rabbits reproduce mythically, the people, hardly at all. This leached soil, the rabbit's hearth, is the farmer's despair.. Endless stone walls indicate how many of his fields were once bailiwicks of rock. Many of them still are: the top soil is too absurd, and the rock movers are too few and far between, and above all, too old.

"This last place God made." One hears that crack repeated at the expense of nearly every locality in the West at one time or another. Indeed, an abundance of farmers are reluctant to credit the nonsense of an American moon landing; the photographs of the moon's surface too closely image lunar landscapes where they have gone themselves in search of missing sheep. "I thought it was as grand a picture as ever I seen," one is told, "but it was a hill, a hill or a mountain, not the moon."

Once these lands were so far from the center of things, they *were* the center of things; their inhabitants included the most literate men in all of Europe, those pastoral monks who exported their learning to the rest of Europe, only to find the favor returned through invasions by savage types as the Normans and the Danes. Later, the Lord Protector Oliver Cromwell — whose dour face Thomas Carlyle called "the kindest . . . Ireland ever saw" — gave the Irish who survived the effects of his psalm-wielding soldiery the Hobson's Choice of Hell or Connaught. Beneath this offer lurked a joke which, like most Puritan jokes, was designed to be unfunny; namely, that the geography west of the River Shannon was just barely distinguishable from the devil's own province. The defeated Irish remnants dragged themselves to Connaught, to Kerry, and to the Burren of Clare, that region commonly said to lack the wood to hang a man, the water to drown him, and the soil to bury him. Even today, the Irish countryman ranks Cromwell on a scale of civility somewhere below his pigs. "He was the evilest person that ever lived," says one small farmer. "If I had been living in his time, I wouldn't have been seen dead at a pig fair with him." This man has not read history to reach this conclusion. Nor has he heard of Thomas Carlyle.

Thanks to celibacy, emigration, and absentee holdings, this derelict geography can again boast a high concentration of learning, as it did in the time of the monks. At the moment, it isn't book learning, though. It is the sort of learning that is gleaned from listening hard with every ear. For this is the domain and last known habitat of the men who it is said "have the old tales." These men lived up snaggle-stoned mountains, on the far sides of islands, down arthritic peninsulas, hedged on blenched farms in remote glens, and fixed on tongues of earth twisting through granite boulders. Places where the hounds of progress can't stray so readily: they'd get corns on their treadmill feet.

Here, the spirit of place rises up from inanimate things. Outspewings of rock are the brains of the soil, the brains of the sea. The upstart machine stands condemned for its constitution of fragile bric-a-brac. Televisions suffer lingering, inscrutable deaths; once in a while, one finds them thrown into bog holes in disgust. The telephone dissolves in the night only to resurrect itself the next morning bearing four conversations simultaneously. The motorcar has the durability of Belfast: an overworked donkey leads an easier life. The tinsel Morris Minor must negotiate the worst western roads with the manic futility of a fly stuck in treacle. In Connemara, a farmer's stony acres, often tilted on the side of a mountain, turn the tractor into a Ruth amid the alien corn. Only the portable radio, the medium of hand-held speech, seems to escape unscathed. And the camera also survives, photographing it all.

And yet, from these ungenerous lands have emerged rare, secret provisions, canny styles of survival, a vigorous folklore, and lovely human utterance; recompense, perhaps, for the fact that life was deposited there in the first place. The spartan bareness of landscape has often inspired a prodigality of personality in people; it has given them something to will away with words. The answer is clearer than any weather such people could possibly know: take away this gray land, and they will be nothing. "Like a lot of people from here, I went to work in Birmingham, in England," says a "returned" Galway man. "But the funny thing was, though we all lived together, we never talked to one another. Or but very seldom. We were all sort of . . . paralyzed. We'd hardly ever greet each other in the streets, in the pubs, or in the churches. So I came back here."

Perhaps the imagination feeds on austerity, like the dryas and gentian found in remote western places, which require a starvation diet in order to flourish. "A good story fills the belly" runs an old Irish proverb. And one wonders, can words actually sustain life? There are tribes in Ghana who believe that they can hold up the spirit of a dying man indefinitely just by breathing words, as if they were living substances, through his lips. This special verbal resource differs a little from "the pure thick wit" possessed by the Kerry storyteller Seán O'Conaill, "and not just out of his mouth, all over him and in his *eyes,* too," says a man who heard him nearly fifty years ago. But Seán O'Conaill and an African practitioner of word magic are of the same cloth. Their words are therapeutic: the difference is only in degree. Many a man was conveyed through a lean season by O'Conaill's tales.

The storyteller is a heroic figure. I can't rid myself of that notion. I can't rid myself of the image of an old man with no formal education and with the grace of language, beside the proverbial turf-fire (an oil-burning radiator will not do), reciting an intricate wonder tale, which he'll call a *sénchas* (history), to an enthralled group of his neighbors. The man who had heard Seán O'Conaill describes such sessions in this way: "The people in it were so quiet, you could hear the snipe in the bog and he not far from quiet hisself."

After this full quiet, the media gods. Western audiences have switched images, and they now prefer the television *shanachie* Eamon Kelly (if not *The Little House on the Prairie*), despite the fact that it's still possible to hear Kelly's stories told in person by some of the same people from whom he first heard them.

Even a malfunctioning television can be a thing of great and blinding beauty: like Halley's Comet cut down in size and imprisoned in a box. Irish television (Radio Telefís Eireann) first arrived on New Year's Eve in 1961. Audiences to the east, in Dublin and Leinster, were able to get the BBC from across the Irish Sea prior to that date; but their identities, given their habitat "within the Pale," had long since been established by attitudes not unlike those presented on British television. Beyond this paleness, however, audiences were treated to the spectacle of glossy, fantastic images from outer space for the first time, and it didn't take them long to decide that they preferred American situation comedies over programs having to do with their own culture. It was like opting for cleanliness over dirt and grime. And they were just as enchanted by *The Late, Late Show* and its host Gay Byrne, who is urbane and, well, cosmopolitan. Halley's Comet began its perpetual sweep around their houses, even while the moon lay just outside their doors, across a few fields and maybe a bog.

Academic folklorists never tire of advancing the theory that each new generation creates its own traditions: that compelling new forms are taking the place of compelling old ones all the time. But nothing has taken the place of storytelling, least of all a graceless machine whose rites are observed in the privacy of one's own home. Even so, television is no more than the end product — or final villainy, perhaps — of a long process of looking to other worlds for sustenance. Already by the 1920's, Seán O'Conaill had lost his own audience. Herding his few cattle, he'd practice his stories to a stone wall, the better to remember them should anyone happen to be interested. And this conversation between a man and the wall that divides his small holdings remains the story of the West even today.

Old man, memory man, man of words, you will never be young again.

The Shanachie

My rhymes more than their rhyming
tell
Of things discovered in the deep. . . .
—— W. B. Yeats, "To Ireland in
the Coming Times"

Mackerels Was All Me Life

. . . and sitting by the fire one of them cried out, "Michael Hart, can you tell a story?" "Never a one," said I. On that he caught me by the shoulders and put me out like a shot.
— "A Fairy Entertainment" told by Michael Hart
in W. B. Yeats's *Irish Fairy Tales*

Arra, man, it is the way with them now, they have shoes on them as soon as they can crawl, not to mention all the clothes they wear, for all that they are weak, and will be.
— Maurice O'Sullivan, *Twenty Years A-Growing*

THE PENINSULA OF CORCA Dhuibhne ("The Spawn of the Goddess"), in the County Kerry, is a narrow spine of mountain pounded on its two sides by the bays of Dingle and Tralee. Its special atmosphere, wrote Cyril Connolly, "is expectant and devotional, like Iona or Delphi." Maybe, but most of its votaries these days are tourists with cameras, capturing its blue distances. The Slieve Mish Mountains ("The Phantoms") fortify the peninsula against the rest of the country; someday, if the shoals of Castlemaine Harbor continue to spread, it will be an island, like the Great Blasket, suspended at the westernmost end of its snout. Across the sound from the Blasket is Mount Eagle, which becomes Slea Head with an impetuous, inhuman slope. To the north is the promontory of Sybil Head, and The Three Sisters, presiding like great stone Fates over the entrance to Smerwick Harbor. Mount Brandon, Saint Brendan's corrie-molded peak, rises far to the other side of the harbor; on a clear day, the view from the top, where the Saint himself fasted, indicates that the prospective faster need not be without some sustenance after he's renounced the crutch of food. Farther still, visible across Dingle Bay, the corrugated draperies of Macgilli-cuddy's Reeks, with the lofty Carrantuohill ("The Left-Handed Reaper"), pattern the Iveragh peninsula. From Dingle, their supernal loveliness (more "spawn" from the goddess?) promises that when this world dies, it will be with the click of a Kodak, instead of a bang or a whimper. In fact, all that the future can promise with certainty is the camera tearing loudly through these mountains.

In Dingle town, I make inquiries about the existence of local storytellers. It is an odd sensation, to ask for a storyteller. Here is a happy array of commercial establishments, a business center of a thousand mostly industrious people, and I am trying to locate an item of small, utterly unmercantile value. Baffled looks alternate with a suggestion that I might save myself the trouble by purchasing a book of Irish stories, retold by a writer at the cost of only *eighty new pee.*

"I hate stories, and I wouldn't listen to one if you paid me. Stories didn't do this country one bit of good," says the propri-etor of the Irish crafts shop. His manner is not unkind, given the coolness of prosperity in his voice. But in that voice, there is a distinctly cautionary note, such as a man might adopt to guard state secrets: one false move might undo all the good work of the E.E.C. (the European Economic Community), not to men-tion exposing fulsome bog odors in unlikely places.

This man has purged his own shop of all odors, the better to meet the eclectic tastes of tourists cleanly. It is a tourist's platonic idea of a crafts shop. There are Donegal linens and pullovers, a selection of Aran knitwear, O'Casey plays, silver Kilkenny torques, Waterford crystal, fleece-lined knickers from Cork, Connemara pottery, Ordnance Survey maps, jewelry, Scottish shortbreads, and a rack of etchings, one of which depicts a pipe-smoking beldam (self-consciously beldamic) in front of her thatched hut, another showing a grizzled man posed in bawneen waistcoat and cleated brogues by his hearth, entitled "The Storyteller Begins His Tale." "The Storyteller Begins the Beguine" it might just as well have been called, for in a surreal fashion, this man has been bedizened with fleece-lined knickers from far-off Cork.

The crafts seller mentions a retired fisherman named Tomás Walsh living near the village of Ballyferriter. Tomás might have the odd tale, but then again, he mightn't. He's still alive, that is fairly certain. An old-age pensioner. Charming gent, and a bit arthritic.

The man dashes out to remove his rack of postcards from the sidewalk: the rains, the storied Kerry rains, have begun to fall.

The little cabins (they are called "cottages" only if they are going to be sold to an English person) herd loosely on the hillside. Through the muslin of rain, they resemble shards of an irreclaimable civilization. In one of them lives Tomás Walsh, but which one? Trying to find the right place, I get lost in an entanglement of *boreens*. These fuchsia-lined roads intimate a diminutive, delicate order, like the veins of a leaf. "Road," indeed, is only a euphemism for what seems actually more like pre-Adamite tracks for cattle.

I stop at a house, a new County Council bungalow, to ascertain where it is Tomás Walsh lives, and to distinguish him from the rest of his clan — this is Walsh country — I utter: "The storyteller."

The man at the door studies me as if I am enlisting his support for a cattle raid. At certain moments, I figure, the countryman and his dialectical opposite, the seller of country crafts, must share the same kidney. This man has taken on the impermeability of a stone wall. Suddenly, the earth has become a crabbed place for him.

"You're not a Munster man," he says after a silence. He has just looked to my shoes. There is little dried cow dung adhering to them.

As I prepare to plead guilty to this accusation, his face jettisons its suspicion and he is all brightness and light. Of course, *now* he understands. He had thought I had been mocking *him*. Tagging *him* with "storyteller." A dealer in falsities. For he is Tomás Walsh, Tomás *Pats* Walsh; the man I want is Tomás Tom Walsh, an older man living just the fields of four cows over; sure, that was the difficulty, sheer coincidence, the wrong Tomás Walsh, he had thought he had been abused, because "you can't walk around calling people 'storytellers,' t'isn't safe nor healthy." He makes this last point half-whimsically (the other half has the seriousness of Linus Pauling brooding over the common cold). A defensiveness, a desire to be pleasant, settles over him now, and he almost shouts to be heard above the loud rustle of the rain in the furze. No; yes; Tomás Walsh, the other one, the old fisherman, you could try him, he might have the odd story, but the kind of man you want is as dead as the golden eagle ...

If storytellers are fleeced with knickers in shops, then in County Council bungalows, all of whose three designs are the same, they are taken to be purveyors of deception. There must be some precise connection between buildings and the furnishings of words their rafters condone, for I heard of one old storyteller who forgot his entire repertoire, after he had been delivered from his Connemara cabin to a glassy hotel, and spent two hours discussing the weather in a futile attempt to dredge up just one story for the visiting folklorist. Afterward, he confessed he had never been among so many windows in his life and that all of them together in the one spot brought hopeless confusion to his talents. His own three-room house had a degree of personal comfort that made this new hotel seem like a hutch for Huns by comparison.

Perhaps like whiskey, a certain sort of person ages best the closer he is to the moist ground. Perhaps dampness is the sap of a certain sort of life. When I reach Tomás Walsh's cabin at last, I can see that it is close to the ground; with the erratic low brow of its base, it appears in fact to be a projection from the same ground off which it has taken its roughly shaped stones, hugging it in return for this gift.

"De bheath-sea." Brigid, Tomás Walsh's wife, presses my hand. "Come in and welcome."

She leads me inside, into the center room, where everything seems to be pulled toward the large stone hearth with a turf fire in it. This hearth would be large enough to seat an entire family, though now there is only a stippled sheep-dog sleeping in front of it. It would be large enough to hold a storyteller and his listeners.

"Dia's Muire dhuit," Tomás greets me. His oyster-gray eyes, however, are riveted to the perfervid figures his television exhibits hardly two feet away from him. "It does be hard to see," he says, as if in apology. And no wonder, for snow is general all over his screen — sparks of it, endlessly detonating, give the impression of radioactivity to all they touch, which in this case is Telly Savalas, interrogating a mealy-mouthed felon. "Who loves you, baby?"

"I'm gone seventy-six years," says Tomás. He looks like Bertrand Russell at about the same age, except for a wind-clenched quality in his face, a furrowed weathering, the result, he tells me, of fishing nights for mackerel ("Mackerels was all me life"), "the most mysterious of fish, schooling away whole years, and other years, why, there was more than you needed." This is an enigma Lord Russell never had to ponder.

There is a run of advertisements on the television, concluding with a recommendation to view the All-Ireland football final "in the comfort of your own home." I take this opportunity to ask Tomás about his stories, and he begins to talk of his years fishing the west coast of Kerry.

"I loved the sea as a — baby. I was like a person who was born miles away from the sea, who first saw the sea when he was ten year or maybe twenty year of age; but I was practically born in the sea, close to the sea.

"There were two brothers of mine fishing and one day they went away to the States. I went down to the pier one morning, and I had an old bag of books, and I had no use for books at that time, or schooling. You know what I did? I threw them inside the fence, and went out in the curragh, the canoe, and when I came home in the evening, I had a bag of pollocks — the pollocks was my exchange for the books. And you know what I got? An awful slapping from my father, he killed me with the stick. Well, he would have to kill me altogether. The next morning, I hopped out the door without a shoe but wearing a white gansey out of wool. I went down to the pier, and you know, my father knew where I was going and this time, he didn't lay a finger on me.

"It was that way with myself and the sea.

"I gave seven years fishing lobsters. Then I went for the mackerel, the ordinary common mackerel. Sometimes, he was so plentiful — we had an average of six nets — he was so plentiful we couldn't haul in six nets full of him, and we had to get the knife and cut one, or cut two, and let them drift. We were lucky to do that; otherwise, we would be swamped. Our little canoes were too small, too frail, and they would capsize. Now it has happened from Kerry to Donegal, fishermen have lost their life owing to the fact they were too greedy — or maybe they were just lacking in knowledge — they took too many fish, the weather was too rough, the canoe was too small and frail, and they capsized and drowned.

"But it was this way with me, that I was always more at home in a canoe than a motorcar.

"You'd get the mackerel at the dark moon. They put the light in the water. 'Twas nearly useless if the moon was full because the mackerel was intelligent enough to see with his own two eyes what the nets was there as a trap. So you'd want to be crafty, witty, and — cute.

"Fishing is the profession where luck counts the most. It is a hard life. It is a life that the average man today would not do, owing to the hardship. We'd be at it all night and into the morning. We'd often take nothing at all to eat, no tea or nothing, 'twould only weigh us down. The night you hadn't anything to eat, that was the hardest night to catch you. It took hard men to do what the man who's wearing his collar and tie today would not dream of doing. I saw old people, seventy years of age, and they were hale and hearty, perhaps whistling for the night that was ahead of them, arriving at the pier. They had no engines, they had no outboard motors — just their own two oars. Them that's at it now (and around here that's not many anymore, with poaching trawlers from every nation fishing these waters), they're a different race altogether. They take bread, butter, tea, and a gas cooker. And sweetcakes! They're 'Gateaux' fishermen ['Gateaux' is an Irish cake company], that's what I call them.

"So, I had more thanks from the sea than from the school. The sea was a better college. Into a canoe — that's the only college I got.

"Yes, I have stories, and I heard them from other fishermen, older men, while we waited to shoot our nets. And I heard them from the shanachies in their own houses as well. I remember these men well, sitting near the fire, with no pay and no ransom. We had one here who died recently, and when I say recently, I mean twenty-five years ago — Tomás Morley, a good old soul, a harmless creature — who used to leave his home to come to his

friends and to sit down, and a flock of people and myself included sitting around the fire listening to Tomás telling us a
story which lasted two hours. It wasn't boring; if it was boring,
you just left the audience from your place in the middle of the
floor, where there were always too many people and no chairs
provided. There would be fifteen or twenty people there, and
they were listening with their mouths open.

"The shanachies were wonderful company in their own ways,
talking about their own way of life. I make out that they were
better than television, at times, anyways. The best of those old
people, 'twasn't the same program they had going every night at
all. I make out that some of them stories were true, too — stories
about Deirdre and Grainne and all them, 'tis stories like that
happening today, all over. I think woman was the cause of all
the trouble always."

At this, Brigid scolds him mildly with a click of her tongue.
"Who loves ye, baby?" he asks, smiling at her. She is obviously
pleased he has been drawn into this monologue, drawn away,
even momentarily, from "the same program."

"This man has come for a story," she says.

Tomás rises to lay to rest the legendary bald head that goes
shining in the night. His body moves with the slow, attuned
waggle of an eel. Does a man who has spent his lifetime with
the sea at last undulate like one of its creatures? Tomás seems to
have made that ichthyic leap.

Stories? In truth, stories? "I have them all forgot," he protests.
Yet the first thing one notices as he quotes an elliptical fragment
from somewhere and mumbles suggestive titles ("I can't tell 'the
Red-Haired Squint-Eyed Cave-Dweller' anymore"), then defers
to the dead shanachie ("They had the wit, I haven't") and his
own age ("I'm gone seventy-six years"), and swallows innuen-
does to which there is no clue — one notices how much there is
to remember, after all.

It is a stall, nearly a set piece; air must wheeze through the
bagpipes before they can be made to play. Soon he begins to
talk more coherently, offering selected incidents from his own

history, maneuvering away from the prospect of a story like a
hawk circling ever higher above its prey, before plunging down
upon it at last. To Tomás, these particles of memory seem to
create the proper atmosphere for a story; they discover the
archaic past of his youth and connect it, try to connect it, with
the present.

There's millions of pounds of good money spent on
education, and what's the result? They don't know the
difference between a bull and a cow.

— The Tailor, quoted in Eric Cross:
The Tailor and Ansty

His father, Tomás says, knew only two expressions in English,
"Up Tipp!" and "sugar candy." "Up Tipp!" the old man procured
from a traveling ragman who was a fierce Tipperary partisan in
Gaelic football. Concerning "sugar candy," Tomás says his father had a very fuzzy notion of its application. He would use the
phrase indiscriminately to describe the strange civilities of the
English, substituting it whenever he hit upon a native ritual, like
afternoon tea, for which the Irish language would be hard
pressed to find a fit equivalent — "The big landlord was only
after just sitting down to his 'sugar candy' when the servant
brought word of his Queen's death." No one knows how the old
man got this phrase; they don't even know what year he was
born, figuring it to be around the time of the Famine. Tomás
gleams in the reminiscence of his father: "He was a jolly old
man, and he would stay there talking to children as well as to
gray-haired people, he would." But he cannot ever remember
being kissed by him, or by his mother, either. Any gesture of

affection would come through the hands or through the tone of voice. Tomás mentions this small detail with apparent satisfaction.

In his years on the sea, Tomás himself spoke only Irish. "We just talked it with ourselves, and there was no chance for English. I often think that Irish is a language for the sea, like the sea. We called it *deisbhéalach* — 'swift in the mouth,' you know. When you're out the all of the night, you'd need a language like that, that wouldn't make you lonely." After the market for mackerel dried up, he became a landsman and had English thrust on him whether he liked it or not. What the sea confirmed, the land denied, and so he began to wonder if he was speaking the "right" language. Now he knows for sure, and economics, the wind of the cruelest blast, causes him to assail his own language for not being entirely of this world or this time: "Right now I'd give a thousand pounds for English and hang the Irish! I'll give you the root of the tree now. When I go to Tralee tomorrow, I wouldn't get a pint of stout inside in Irish in the bar. I have to stick the Irish in my pocket, and turn on the English. I couldn't sell a cow in Irish, or a sheep. English is the language for making your bit in the world. The Irish is all right between ourselves, but if I go to Boston tomorrow morning, and meet you in the streets, I couldn't speak a word of Irish to you. There."

But Boston does not figure in his immediate plans. He even avoids Tralee, barring visits to his doctor ("I have arthritis from too much wetting"). He cannot walk on land for very long without feeling a sense of trespass; the sea remains his lodestar even now, despite its bringing pain to his body, and that means he won't travel any solid distance unless his health is at stake. A fisherman of his late acquaintance could never affix himself to dry land for more than a few days at a time without growing literally nauseous, "and he'd have to row hisself beyond in the canoe to be well again, do you see." He quotes this story with obvious relish, to prove how open-minded he is by comparison. He has never had the land sickness, exactly.

A portion of his English comes to him through the blizzards of his television. The detective-police programs, imported from America, have a special appeal to him, and he likes to practice some of their flashier idioms, like "How'd you like to have your face changed, runt?" rolling them over in his mouth until he's certain he's got the pronunciation right. He hasn't much use for the Irish language programs of Radio Telefís Eireann (RTE), despite the frequent interviews with cultural remnants somewhat like himself. They are, he says, just like talking with his local friends, "and sure, with them, I can always talk back." Then there is his frustration before any of several alien dialects of Irish: the Connemara and Donegal varieties, and what he calls "Christian Brother's Irish," taught to civil servants in the forlorn hope that someday they will be able to manage their country's bureaucratic duties in its native tongue. If the speaker uses any Irish other than Munster, he might be talking in Serbo-Croat for all Tomás understands of it. There is no King's Irish.

His son, a bachelor of thirty-six, is the other medium through which he has learned the language of his former overlords. Martin has been in Scotland, where he worked as a farm laborer, digging potatoes and bagging them; at the moment, he does seasonal construction work in London, and in the summer, when he returns home, he won't (Tomás says) "speak a word of the Irish," equating it with preposterous backward habits and very little else. Maybe he fears that this craggy speech of his ancestors and of his own father might rise fortuitously to his lips once he returns to an England more and more reticent over the odd ways of the Irish. At any rate, one cannot put up a London scaffolding in Munster Irish. Far too few of Martin's coworkers claim such a language among their skills. Tomás and Brigid do not seem to mind "turning off the Irish" whenever Martin comes home; the language issue pales beside the exigencies of the pay packet Martin posts monthly to supplement their scant old-age pensions.

Further, Martin *reads* — not passionately, not too much, but "the odd book," says Tomás, who finds no fault in books; books

are "learning" like everything else. Save for Harold Robbins's
The Adventurers, which betrays itself by the near naked female
emblazoned on its jacket. This tawdry entertainment is not
learning at all, but "bloody, indecent rubbish." "I wouldn't give
that story to a man but I thought very, very little of him," says
Tomás, who ordinarily saves such imprecations for the feral dogs
that savage his sheep. His own path might never have crossed
Harold Robbins's rutting marks, had he not recently discovered
Martin bent over this novel like a monk scrutinizing an ancient
palimpsest.

"She hadn't as much on her as would stuff a crutch," Tomás
says of the girl on the jacket, in a phrase undoubtedly more
felicitous than anything in *The Adventurers*. He did not, however, read a word of the book. He trusts to the visual précis, and
that is all he knows, all he needs to know. Martin brought the
book over from England, and if *The Adventurers* describes life
over in England, Tomás is not surprised, not at all. For the
English, to his mind, have long since proven their aptitude for
indelicacy. Among other things, they spawned the Black and
Tans, whom he remembers only too well; a drunken member of
that "crowd of murderers," searching local houses for I.R.A.
suspects, vomited on the floor in front of him, in this very house.
He points to the place where it happened. "I was just a young
lad at the time, but I remember it as well as I remember my
name."

When he's told that in fact Harold Robbins comes from the
States, he doesn't believe it. He doesn't believe a writer from the
States would stoop so low as "the dung heap." Nor does he
realize that his television "favorites" are more faithful to the
style of the Black and Tans than one lascivious, used female.

At present, the only two books in the house are surpassingly
strange companions, *The Adventurers* and a missal in Irish.
Doesn't he read novels, though? No, Tomás has never even read
one of *those* "stories." Not that he hasn't the time, or is *altogether* distrustful of their morals, or even too rarely comes
across one (the shops in Dingle, six miles away, sell plenty of

novels). It's just that the novel is a far too recent fashion, compared to the world he inhabits; even though he's no longer in a position to get new ones, it is the stories narrated by the old shanachies that remain his fiction. "A good story would put you into it. The teller might say, 'Now this is a lad that was working by a farmer, and just like *yourself*, Tomás Walsh, he never said the right thing, he always said the wrong thing, whatever thing was over. . . .' Then you were in it, yourself; a part of the story, yourself. I think none of these books could ever do that."

Novels, too, are devoured by a different kind of person: by professors and commuters, housewives and professional people, and fantasists of all persuasions. Here he is, none of these things, attending to the nearly human cries of the pipit. "I do believe myself that when they say they've heard the banshee, they are only just after hearing a bird like him."

Tomás does occasionally read *The Kerryman,* his county organ, but "Listening to me friends was all the reading that ever I done in my life." One realizes that he is content to remain unlettered by ordinary standards. After all, his own type of "learning" goes back — how far? It is difficult to tell with oral knowledge, because of the absence of what scholars call "texts" and what Tomás himself calls "the men with the real wit I knew who had the histories." These men, he says, "are all in the way of truth now. Dead, you see."

For some applications of language, literacy is a nuisance. The ancient Celts discouraged it when they saw it rising up in their court poets. Tomás himself doesn't think he would have kept a single story if he had gotten more than his five years of schooling. "They claim that very educated people don't have memory. Nothing disturbs the mind of the man that doesn't have education." By "memory," he doesn't just mean instant recourse to the minute particulars of his life, "the easy times" and "the hard times" and so on; even book-bound persons retain that facility. Rather, memory fetches to the fore his inheritance of stories, songs, cures, proverbs, and old superstitions, which country people call *pishrogues* ("Tomás is a great one for *pishrogues*,"

says Brigid, "and he doesn't believe never the one of them").
The tatterdemalion remnants, one is tempted to say, the dottle
of a culture such as economical dreams are not made on —
unless by stage actors.

What can be done nowadays with the somewhat unsanitary
practice ("in my grandfather's time, mind you, and before") of
applying moss from a human skull to an open wound, thus to
close it?

Or the belief that "the old people were supposed to be pray-
ing for a soul in Heaven when they was smoking their pipes"?

Or that "bad jaundice they thought could be cured of you if
you only drunk a jar — a pint mug — of your own urine and
then fasted for six days"?

Or "if ye just threw an old shoe at a man after he's left the
house, all that man's children will be good, strong, and
healthy"?

Or that "a man named O'Sullivan, *any* man by that name,
could cure the gout"?

Or that "the people in Connaught speak that way [very husk-
ily] because long ago they stole Saint Patrick's goat and ate
him"?

Or "if you do be always waving a hazel rod over your head,
nothing can harm you"?

Or . . . he goes on and on, and a curious, recondite poetry
begins to take form; a frowsy artistry, deep from the cairn of
rural identity. "Them things, well, we used to recite them at
night to keep ourselves awake during the mackerel season."
"Them things" are fragile and innocuous compared to the more
modern belief that atoms can be split.

After reeling off these *pishrogues*, Tomás chuckles. They provide the substance for a cool, remembering humor. He knows
they are absurd, but he has them here in his head in all their
steadfast absurdity, hasn't he? "There were many things like
that going when I was a lad. The old people, it was all that kind
of stuff all through their lives, fairies and *pishrogues*. You know

what put an end to all that? The fight for freedom in 1916. I was there meself, meself and a neighbor behind, they're all . . . scattered now. We'd have our time watching the Tans. Before the Tans, we were looking for the pookah man. You know the pookah man? The Tans put us right. And now there is no pookahs today — the only pookahs today is girls and boys going together all night."

Brigid protests (maybe she wants to divert the conversation from the subject of nocturnal trysts, too). *Some* of the old cures did work, perhaps not the sort that required the seventh son of a seventh son trampling the side of your neck to cure the pains there, but take nettles, for example: "The juice of the nettle will cure stomach wind and asthma if you mix it with milk. And I seen a man with terrible rheumatism, and I seen him getting two of the boys here last year. He stripped, and they got two big bunches of nettles, and they beat him, and they beat him for half an hour, and I don't believe he had the rheumatism pain since. It took the whole lot out of him. Well, it's not everyone who'd put up with the nettles."

Nor does she believe the fight for freedom removed the banshee with much efficiency: "The fairies may be gone, but the banshee is still in it. She has been heard here on a few occasions, I remember, and a very mournful wail she has. Well, a lot of people believe she is some member of the family come back when another member would be dying, and she comes wailing, after that particular person, that is their idea. I heard the banshee myself, crying here."

Tomás will not abide by the banshee even though he knows that Brigid will stick to her till her dying day. " 'Tis birds, only night birds," he asserts;

"No night bird wails like that," she replies.

Yet, despite this contention that she is from the birds, the banshee seems likely to prevail for another generation among the Walshes. Martin has heard her in London, near Charing Cross. He was flustered enough to place a long distance call to the local parish priest; no, the priest said, as far as he knew, neither of Martin's parents had been struck down by recent illness. This is a faith that leaps across seas.

The banshee is really the last of the old *pishrogues* to die out. Fairies and their kin may come and go, and only the "delicate" imagine that "it is all over," as Tomás puts it, "if you meet a turkey by night"; but it will take at least another western generation astounded by other sounds to quell the banshee's wailing. The wonder is, that it remains possible to prick an ear during a television advertisement for Youghal carpets and hear the same sound Brian Boru heard, informing him he'd go to his death at Clontarf. Perhaps this plaintive sound — and it is no more than that — inhabits the realm of possibility; one day, it may increase to a scrutable word, and the word is, or was, an aid to the melodious asperity of this life.

A people with a feel for the delights of human talk let their doorsteps rot with green moss; they are not very concerned with what they see, only with what they hear. And so they grant ruins a staunch visibility in their countryside, where the ruins are the most ruinous in Europe. In the towns, these ruins are razed and replaced with the plasticated branch offices of the Energy Supply Board, which tax the natural art of listening. A person must sharpen his ears considerably before he can hear the tread of board officials sinking softly into the Youghal carpeting.

Tomás begins to talk about an ancestor who had gotten himself killed in Scotland during the last rout of the clans in 1746. This man "went up to Scotland to fight the English," sinking his own meagerness into the forces of the Heather Prince. Though there are no records to prove it, Tomás thinks this man was killed at Culloden. "He was the rambling type of man, I heard my father say. He was an old bagpipe musician, he was, and I think he went to Scotland to play his pipes on the battlefield. That was always the traditional place to play them." The event gathers an immediacy on his lips, as if he were regarding a friend's corpse laid out before him, performing a postmortem on the man's life for whatever logic of behavior it will yield. "He was related to the Carneys on my father's side, and they came from Murreigh, and they were always fine musicianers."

Memory dies hard with Tomás. Advancing age seems to refine rather than nullify it. Almost, his thoughts preclude the past; the present increases to a single complex simultaneity. "It is traditional in the Irish race to remember this stuff," he says. And many generations before him, he has the instructive example of the Irish king injured in the Battle of Moira in 646. That king was hit such a severe blow to his head that, according to the chronicler of the event, "his brain of forgetting was stricken out of him." No matter how diligent his attempts after that, he could forget nothing. So he decided to put all his remembrances down in poetry.

Let us go forth, the tellers of tales, and seize whatever prey the heart longs for, and have no fear. Everything exists, everything is true, and the earth is only a little dust under our feet.
— W. B. Yeats, *The Celtic Twilight*

"I will tell a short piece, in Irish," Tomás says.

Perhaps he can be persuaded to narrate an old wonder tale, about Finn McCool, say, or Cuchulainn, or one of the old kings of Ireland?

"I'm not a poet. You'd need a poet for it. You'll never get a fiannaíocht story [one that concerns the Fianna, Finn McCool's warriors] from anyone but a poet, for a poet is a gifted man. He might never go to school, but he'd be a poet, himself. Three things you can't learn — you'll never learn to be wise, you'll never learn to be good-hearted, and you'll never learn to be a poet. Those things come from breeding. Education, too, comes from breeding. You might have two well-educated brothers, and you might have four more brothers, and the Devil mightn't educate them.

"My story begins this way: More years ago than I can tell you or you can tell me, when the roads of Ireland were paved with pennyloaves and the streets of Dingle were paved with gold blocks, there were some fishermen once who set out in a boat, a very big boat, a tall-masted boat . . ."

As I listen to this story, my eyes wander to a copy of *The Kerryman* neatly folded by the open hearth. A pair of spectacles rests on an open page, where boldface type announces: **Space-age Electronics Arrive in Kerry Gaeltacht.** The accompanying photograph shows a young woman examining the finished circuit card design from a computer.

Tomás has begun the story with every sign of conviction, and his voice is musical in its enthusiasm for the remote truths he is divulging; Irish, which he has used only in occasional phrasings until now, is a pride and a delight in his mouth.

The outline of the story itself is quite clear: the fishermen are the old sort who take to the sea for days at a time, bringing with them all of their possessions and their women . . . after a time, these fishermen realize they are being followed by a sea-serpent . . . to appease this rather terrifying creature, they throw it wool, then a spinning wheel, and at last, the spinning woman herself . . . the serpent devours this rich feed and swims away, apparently satisfied . . . time passes, and the fishermen are blessed with plentiful catches . . . more time passes, and the serpent is washed up dead on a shingly strand where people are gathering seaweed for manure . . . the woman is found spinning away inside the creature's gut . . . and she blasts her rescuers for interrupting her work.

Before reaching the end, however, he has begun to hear other music, and the frank moment when the woman curses her captors, the story's *pièce de résistance,* he speeds through as if it were an unwelcome wad of phlegm to be dispatched from his throat. I notice his foot tapping before I hear the music that has prompted it — an exotic song, fitful and languorous, that a Berber shepherd is playing on his primitive pipe.

Brigid had turned the television back on to view a documentary on the Berbers of North Africa. First, she was content with the picture alone, but then she was so intrigued by it that she turned up the sound a little, then a little more, and finally, much louder than she imagined. The demands of strangeness are seductive and forceful, and a people in the midst of a cultural sea-change, like these Berbers, are perhaps more strange because of it.

On the screen, a scrofulous-looking boy, with bell-bottom trousers, is reciting passages from the Koran. While a burnoosed sheikh is fixing the flat tire of his hauling van, his wife, her forehead tattooed with ink dots, peers out shyly from the back of the van. The punctilious BBC narrator speaks of vanishing Bedouins, vanishing traditions and observances, and even a kif that isn't as good as it used to be (though maybe like Oscar Wilde's Oxford, it never was as good as it used to be).

"I got that story from Micheál Keane, and he's been dead for twenty years or more, and he heard it from his father, and I don't know how far back it goes before that, to the days of the sea serpents maybe. I got that story one night when we — Micheál and meself and two Manning brothers, they're all dead and gone now — were at the nets," says Tomás, just as the BBC man is comparing the sustaining qualities of kif to the coca chewed by the people of the Andes.

We have our dinner of cabbage and boiled bacon in front of the television, and soon after the tea is served, some of the Berber tribesmen begin to lunch on a spring lamb, in front of their cavernous tent. "My grandfather lived to near a hundred years old, and ate only spuds, 'twas spuds all through his life,"

Tomás says a little defensively. The video lamb on a spit has led him to support his native dish, when otherwise he would have probably disparaged it as the capricious staple of poverty. For he has concluded that these bedraggled mountain people are better off than their counterparts in his own country. The Irish farmer's profit is in the marketing, not the eating, of his livestock.

But soon the steep foothills of the Atlas Mountains elicit his sympathies: "The fresh air is the best life for anyone that's used to it." "Fresh air," in his unraveling of that sentence, becomes a circumstance not everyone can endure: a lifetime where nothing was easy is infused with it. Yet these North Africans, so different in most respects from his own people in the west of Ireland, have managed, from the look of the rocks on which they live, to capture his creaturely respect. Suddenly, this bleak African world has become his own: geography runs deeper in him than styles of eating. Neither Dublin nor Tralee could have inspired this kind of alliance.

Then the news reports an outbreak of fresh violence in Belfast. A Protestant schoolboy has been gunned down by the Provos; also, a Protestant judge; also, a U.D.A. man inside a supermarket. And the television screen exhibits the wrenched face of a Catholic mother of four whose husband has just been shot in a suburb of Belfast for alleged Republican sympathies. "It must be a different world, a different world," Tomás says to me. "In my own day . . ." he begins, but he is interrupted in midsentence by the weather report, "Showers in Munster and South Leinster, heavy and prolonged in places, and bright spells." After this last revelation, we watch *Chad Hanna*, with the young Henry Fonda, followed by an interview with a country bachelor who is looking for a wife to share the burden of his farm chores. In the distance, the camera catches, though not intentionally, a ram mounting a ewe.

The later it is in the evening, Tomás tells me, the clearer his television screen is.

Tomás walks with me to his gate, and suddenly, a dog's lone bark quickens to a raucous chorus of barking from all the dogs on all the small farms in the surrounding area. They're like that now, says Tomás. Now that people are spending more of their evenings inside, the dogs aren't used to steps in the night. Each footfall is potentially a stranger's.

The drizzle has developed into a slashing rain. "It's as wet as shite," Tomás says, and tries to make it back to his house before getting too wet. But in the West, they call this "spiritual weather." In the end, it is "spiritual weather" that does in a man's work.

I Only Want to Possess
What I Have

O Gaelic, most sweet and soft of sound,
Swift, robust, as the waves of the sea,
Trodden and trampled, despised by all —
That you live at all is a wonder to me!
 — Peadar O Doirnín (1704–1764)

ALONG THE ROAD to Ballinskelligs, where Seán Murphy lives, the rain has released the sweet breath of whin blossoms. Painted green on the wall of a byre, the manifesto **NO E.E.C.** has been nearly expunged by this watery persistence — only the **NO**, sprayed directly beneath the jutting roof, remains distinct, a meaningless negation. A porridgy fog shrouds the islands in the bay and the surrounding mountains with a thick invisibility.

It has been raining here for quite some time, as long, Seán

Murphy says, "as a wet Sunday." Yet he is out in his fields nevertheless, administering a homemade preparation of meal and herbs to a heifer taken sick from eating the toxic wort-weed. " 'Tis an odious fine day," he says, looking up from the medicinal pail and composing his mouth to a wry smile that perfectly dramatizes these paradoxical words. Then he returns to the heifer, speaking gently to it in Irish, with his face near its ear, describing the joy of its imminent recovery. A tumble of adjectives catalogues the delights of the chalky mixture he is feeding it; there could be but few people who'd dispose him to the lyrical resources of his own language like this. "This cow has no English," he says.

The pectoral muscles swell beneath his linen shirt as he force-feeds the animal. His hard, classical features, with just the suggestion of an aquiline nose, undermine every equation of age with appearance. At sixty-five, he looks at least fifteen years younger; his neighbors say that with each passing year, he is actually *looking* younger. The rich gusty air of the Atlantic is supposed to be aphrodisiacal in these parts. It seems to enhance the liveries of age for those men and women it does not wizen prematurely with its knife-edged winds.

This is "the place of the Skelligs," the place from which pilgrims once departed for Skellig Michael, "the most Western of Christ's fortresses in the ancient world," to do austere penance on that Gothic fang ten miles into the Atlantic off the Kerry coast. The other Skellig, Little Skellig, is the second largest breeding ground for gannets in the Northern Hemisphere.

One story has it that all madmen in Ireland, if left to their own devices, would bear straight to these two lunar pyramids in the ocean. At present, however, there are only sightseers and gannet fanciers, and they take the easier sea route to the Skelligs from Valentia Island, which leaves Ballinskelligs to "the language people" (as Seán calls them), students "at the Irish" and journalists swotting up the language, prideful bearers of the *Fainne*, the gold ring that is the insignia of a speaker of Irish. Seán himself has addressed Irish language classes here on whatever comes to his mind, whether folklore, Kerry poets like Tomás Roe O'Sullivan or Owen Roe O'Sullivan, or "the way of life we had in the Gaeltacht long ago." He wears his feelings with complete restraint, and so his amusement is polite and amiable when he is reminded that he may have something to say to these summering fugitives from the cities. He is proud of his language and its culture, of course. But his grin of pride also bespeaks a perplexity: where (it asks) was this attention, and the stipends for native Irish speakers, and the government grants to small farmers, when the people really needed such bolstering? Nor does he really understand why Irish, though a beautiful language, deserves anyone's fanatical attitudinizing. "I speak a language which no one ever gave a thought or care about. They spoke it like churning the butter; it was like churning the butter, that's all."

But it isn't really *all*, for this same language once made criminals of its speakers, which butter churning never did. Seán cites one incident from his own youth: "Around the time of the 'Troubles,' we weren't allowed to use the Irish for any public writing. My father had a little ass and cart, and there was an edict here by the British Constabulary — you might call them the Royal Irish Constabulary — that you must have your name in English on each vehicle and an ass and cart is a vehicle under the law, and 'twas the only vehicle we had at that time. So wasn't I the right rogue, and didn't I carve my father's name on the shaft of the ass and cart — in Irish! My father was fined the sum of ten shillings at the local court, and afterwards, he called me a bastard for it." Today, the situation is ironic many times over. This felonious Irish is the language of prestige for non-Irish-speaking localities, especially Dublin; and in the Gaeltacht regions, those remote enclaves of tradition and indigence, English is the language of prestige and under its auspices only does the word "dollars" (which means a plushy job, anywhere) makes sense.

Of course, the older denizens of the Gaeltacht who are still on speaking terms with their neighbors will continue to speak Irish with them, but when these people die, as Seán says, "the language as we know it will be buried with them." A young girl, a student, passes his way, and to illustrate this last point, he addresses her in Irish, "When was the last time you said the rosary in the evening?" She shrugs uncomprehendingly and passes on with as much grace as her platform shoes permit her on this pebbly road.

"The language will be buried with them," Seán reiterates with a certain nonchalance, nearly as though the stony silences of the West had seeped into his prophecy, rendering it emotionless. He is feeding his heifer more easily now. A cry in torrential Irish or the bleating of a sheep comes down the mountain behind him, no, it is a sheep, one of Seán's lambs wanting its mother. Higher up comes a staccato of reassuring bleats, and all's well in one, albeit precipitous, world. And it really is precipitous, for Seán does not own land, he owns mountain, and his chores are a quotidian tilt with existence. Yet, knowing no other world, he respects this one. What he's never had, he's never missed. The same thing can be said for any person living anywhere else, too: for Londoners, for aborigines.

A wooden clatter heralds the return of the girl with platform shoes. She totters down the road, sidestepping fresh cow dung. She nods, gravely, as she passes, her coat pockets provisioned with sweets for the Irish language course directly before her. "When was the last time you were at Confession?" Seán asks her, again in Irish. Thinking she has been mocked, she tosses her head; her hauteur is suddenly her chariot, and she rides it away. Seán pursues her with the leisurely gaze of the small farmer on a wet day. "I'd sooner have an acre of hay down in bad weather than have that one down and on her back in any kind of weather," he says. Then he goes up the crenulated slope of the hill with his donkey and cart, to haul down turf. When he arrives back, his laden cart makes less clamor than the pair of platform shoes on the road.

Died in the Parish of Aglish, in the vicinity of Killarney at the very advanced age of 115 years, Theodore O'Sullivan, the celebrated Irish Bard. This extraordinary man, who was a great composer in his native language, expired suddenly on Wednesday last, whilst sowing oats in the field of one of his great-grandchildren. The deceased was also a cooper, and is said to have made a churn from which butter was taken for the christening of his 26th great-grandchild.

— Obituary Notice in *Freeman's Journal*,
March 4, 1820

Like Tomás Walsh, Seán Murphy can tell stories in the traditional manner. But his "wit" (as Tomás would call it) is something else, coming from other realms. Perhaps it is stimulated by all those mountains: living perpetually among them may exalt one's word-wisdom. Mountain people, more than their lowland and oceanic brethren, have perforce to improvise and scheme to drive hunger from their doorways.

Mountains contain stories the same as the interlocking lives of people. In fact, there is a legend that beneath one of the mountains just behind Seán's house sleeps a whole cavalry of wild horsemen. They are awaiting the local equivalent of the Day of Judgment, and then, they will awaken to wreak havoc on the enemies of the Catholic faith. Seán has an instinctive feel for the numinous, but he doesn't exactly believe this story. No, the place this Apocalypse will happen, he heard, is Slieve-nan-Or, in the County Galway.

Also, Seán has never seen fit to invest in a television. There is a practical reason for this. "I can't see sitting in front of a piece of furniture all the time," he says. "You could just as well watch a chair for an evening. Or look at the television from the other side." It is a question of hygiene as well. "I wouldn't know now but the television mightn't do harm to the brains or to the vision. Well, I'm certain it would, the television." The old culture can be witnessed in him through the fervor of his belief in those last words.

Tomás Walsh would probably defer to Seán as a shanachie. According to Tomás, poetry separates the shanachie from the man who only "has" a story and will tell it if he's asked. Those who do not have this poetry might just as well not bother. Those who do have it reserve it for the wonder tales, the most lyrical of all the old Irish survivals; it was difficult to know for sure, but Tomás might indeed have known some of them, but to tell them, as he himself said, "to tell them if you wasn't a poet born and bred would be a bloody cod." So Tomás refused to tell them.

"A man knows he's a poet," says Seán, who would never agree to the conjunction of his name with that calling, "like he knows his own fields, which his father had, and his grandfather." The consequence of breeding, is it? Or the consequence of — *farming?*

"He's in Dublin, he's in Cork, no, no good," asserts Seán. "When you go to those places, and to the States, you won't have your histories, and you mightn't even have your own name, because you're looking, you're talking, and you're walking and they go out of your head, out like the rain from the clouds. But we're free here, out in the open, and I make out that that's the reason we have them in memory, you see. The noise and racket going to a city, you won't have them at all. You go to a public house and some of them wants a song and more of them wants a drink, and you don't know where you are.

"I heard them say on the wireless you had to be born in a city, or a town, to be well-educated and have it, d'you see, but I believe myself that the best breed of a person will come from the most backward parts of the world, in fact, from the deserts, the best."

The country, or "the deserts," versus the city is not a line of reasoning he wishes to pursue, however. Dialectics is not his métier. He'd rather discuss the more palpable life of his own fields. Or the rooks settling in a tree, "just there now, look, like tea leaves." That is a subject he will remark upon.

"He sings to his sheep," a girl in the village says of Seán, and giggles. There's an end to it as far as she is concerned. She might think that singing to sheep is an especially backward way of talking to yourself. But the status of the shanachie is predicated on the necessity of an audience, and sheep are, if less responsive and dumber than most, at least an audience. Seán guesses he has not held an actual storytelling session in thirty years. Not that it really matters, he indicates, not that they are more than mere bagatelles, "but I have those grand old histories about the Fianna and the Red Branch Knights, and I have them now as good as ever I did. They say that when the times goes between yourself and those things, those stories — you don't tell them for years, and then they're better, when you tell them. They say that they improves with the person's age, too. I heard Seán O'Conaill at a *feis* and in his own house when he was eighty years of age and there was a lot in his stories that a younger man wouldn't have. Oh yes, that is so. He was from this part of Kerry, you know."

Often lavished on men like Seán are jeremiads about mute inglorious Miltons, thwarted ambitions, and opportunities lost somewhere between the idea and the conception. If only this poor beleaguered half-life were born elsewhere, so it is said, he might have developed into another James Joyce, another Einstein, another Viscount Montgomery or at the very least, another academic. Seán himself is impervious to this sort of rhapsodizing. From his own point of view, Einstein and the rest of them would be the talents gone to waste, the men born in the forlorn places. For him, it is the quality of life, not accomplishment, that matters most, and in that sense, who knows, Einstein might well have been better off if he had been born, and remained, in Ballinskelligs.

I ask Seán if he thinks he might have actually *written* poetry if he had been born elsewhere. "We have a saying here," he says, " 'Put mouth to mouth, but never put pen to paper.' "

"And I wouldn't have been born elsewhere but here, either, in these townlands. If I was, I'd still be — a farmer, a small farmer. It's the best life of all. This land is no good for tillage, but the best grassland there is, and one acre of land here can nearly feed a cow, and that cow gives a thousand gallons of milk, now.

"I could have gone to the fishing, and my own father worked at fishing, and he worked at the land. Some of them in the village still do a bit of it, Jim Fitz and his sons. But it's hard being a fisherman and having your bitteen of land. You can't whistle and chew meal at the same time. You aren't here, and you aren't there. But the way it is with you, you're trying to be at the land and you're trying to be at the water, and you're only just like the hare when the hound is after her. You're running here, and you're running there, and you have nothing right. So stick to the land, I says, stick to it if ye want to be gathering brains."

So, somewhere, he has misplaced "high endeavor" for servitude to this gray land, which he doesn't reckon to be servitude. "I didn't think it was slavery. Not at all. It was only work, I thought that, and I done it."

He puts this work in the past tense. Although he still does it, or tries to, he holds no romantic illusion that anyone will ever return to *his* land, once he dies, to make it produce again.

"My family have all been living on the land. I have two sons today, but they won't stay on the land. There's no living at all on the land anymore. 'Twould be a complete waste of time asking them to stay on the land. Their future lies in industry."

So: he's using the double standard with his sons. *He'd* still do it, suffer through the small farmer's life again, but not his sons. Or is it that with an upbringing confirmed by hundreds of years of simple subsistence, he just can't imagine himself at anything else, especially this "industry"?

"Farming is all over here. What's keeping them in it still is the few shillings' dole, it's just keeping them struggling. Most of the men here are on the dole, and sure, only for that, they'd die.

"Today, you'd get nothing for half a dozen young calves, let them be six months — you'd have to pay them to take them away for nothing, and you'd have to, because you'd couldn't feed them, either. There was a farmer here a few months back who took his calf to Cahirciveen to sell, and his wife, she asked him to get a chicken in the supermarket for dinner. Imagine that, a farmer in the supermarket! Anyways, he sold the calf for one pound and paid one pound fifty for the chicken. Now two years ago, you would get fifty or sixty pounds for that calf. Well, I'll tell ye, there's no more justice in that than you'd find in the craw of a sick shag."

The smaller the farm, the more difficult it is to live by, and Seán himself owns just under fifty acres, "the land of ten cows" and maybe fifty sheep, he doesn't know for sure, they are forever wandering off or being attacked by dogs, or giving birth. For the first time in his life now, he's forced to contemplate "the cost of living" — at a loss to reconcile it with the old ways, which were never so contradictory as to violate the predicament of living with a word like "cost." The jargon of commercial status is fairly lost on him. It was work, not balance of payments, that a myopic heritage bequeathed to his small farm. How can a man learn to be competitive when his energies are sapped by the occupation of survival? Seán was never destined to have a bank account. His field labor and his rood of tillage "put butter on your bread," and that was all; any concept more abstract than that would cause the mind, Seán's, to grow torpid with disbelief.

"I only want to possess what I have," Seán says.

These days, that particular frail center cannot hold. Constraints within the European Economic Community demand that "farming units" modernize themselves, bloating to a competitive size, or die. Competitive? Seán remembers when men "used to collect Sunday mornings before mass — they wouldn't have the time to come on other days — and they'd sow the potatoes in ridges for the people who couldn't do it theirselves, the widow-women and the old people and the other poor ones. 'Lazy beds' we used to call them. But you wouldn't be lazy to sow them, you had to be lively enough." Then he remembers, and here he catches himself, not just remembers, "we still do it, at the harvesting, a man has a field of hay, like, and there'd be maybe four or five of you from neighboring farms putting that field of hay down, and no shillings offered or wanted, because that is the only way you can get a field down before the winter."

Under the Farm Modernization Scheme, the majority of farms of less than fifty acres get classified as "transitional." How grim the presumption that a man's lineal holdings can become "transitional" in a moment's time, by the mere nodding of a ministerial head! But actually, even this euphemism promises more than it delivers. The farms thus christened are in transit only between the present corporate moment and Nineveh, for which they would appear to be better suited. They are being squeezed out, shabby relics that they are, by the "development" farm, which receives grants boosting it to "commercial status." This second group, it is assumed, can develop "comparable incomes"; that is, incomes equivalent to those received outside the realm of agriculture, in industry and the red-tape professions. Indeed, the whole plan seems designed to transform farmers into bureaucrats before their time. It requests that they keep records of rates and outgoings, of stock land, income, and work hours: such details tell the adjudicator whether the farmer will be able to rise to the "comparable income" of eighteen hundred pounds within four years of time. The farmer must modulate these things into a persuasive letter asking for (in short) help; a hard thing for a person dedicated to self-sufficiency.

Most small farmers think that the targets of this incentive scheme are too difficult for them to meet. And they assume that the keeping of accounts will facilitate a large tax on their small incomes. Himself, Seán observes the custom of not putting pen to paper.

To help "butter the bread," Seán and his two teenaged sons collect periwinkles at the bay for eventual sale to France. "The great peris are twelve shillings sixpence a stone, but of course, you will only pick them when the tide is out. You can pick a hundredweight in eight or nine hours, but you can only work two hours on the strand, while the tide is out — and no pebbles allowed! 'Tisn't too bad, no, not at all."

The fog is lifting, and the blue trunks of Scattery Island and Goat Island are now exposed in the bay, with Bolus Head, which Seán calls "the West" even though it is only six miles away. Always, the tendency is to wish "the West" on someone else.

Seán gazes out on this postcard vista. "Of the forty-two children I went to school with, there's only myself and two other men still in it here," he says.

Now that the rain has nearly stopped, his wife emerges from the house and goes into the adjoining byre to milk the cows. Seán was supposed to do this milking himself, but he has talked right through it. Once, he recalls, "in my time," only the women milked the cows, never the men. The men were not supposed to touch a cow's teat.

"In Cromwell's day, it was 'To Hell or Connaught.' Now it's 'To Hell or Brussels,'" remarks Micheál Murphy, another small farmer living in Ballinskelligs. A younger man than Seán, he is more vehement about the effects of Common Marketeering. "There's so much sameness, fuck it. It makes you start talking to things you should never in your life be talking to. One lad told me that he was talking to the tubs in a meat factory over in England, he had names for them, he was talking to them, he had nothing else."

And this can be carried a step farther. The culture the E.E.C. will market naturally will have to be common, if not downright crude. Even now, there may be teams of Brussels bureaucrats at work on a common European language of four hundred words, each of which pertains to economics. Garreted, starving poets will compose lyrics in praise of high excises. There will be the same songs, the same sperm. And one day, everyone awakening to discover that they look Belgian.

Difference is wanted to make a world. To survive, a man must be able to sing to his sheep before they reach the meat tubs.

You Can Tell My Stories
Aren't Book Stories

Saturday, the 16th of September, 1769, will be sold or set up
for sale, at Skibbereen, the robust horse Spanker, the property
of Thomas O'Donnell, Esq. A strong, staunch, steady, sound,
stout, sinewy, safe, serviceable, strapping, supple, swift, smart,
sightly, sprightly, spirited, sturdy, shining, sure-footed, sleek,
smooth, spunky, well-skinned, sized, and shaped: a sorrel steed
of superlative symmetry, styled Spanker, and a snip square-
sided, slender-shouldered, smart-sighted, with a small star, and
steps singularly stately; free from strain, sprain, spasms, string-
halt, stranguary, sciatica, staggers, surfeit, sealing, sollander, surfeit,
seams, scouring, strangle, strenuous swelling, soreness, scratches,
splint, squint, squirt, scruff, scales, scurp, scars, scabs, scarred
sores, scattering, shuffling, shambling gait or symptoms of sickness of any sort. He is neither stiff-mouthed, shabby-coated, si-
new-shrunk, spur-galled, nor saddle-backed, shell-toothed, slim-
gutted, surbated, skin-scabbed, short-winded, splay-footed, or
shoulder-slipped, and is sound in the sword-point, and stiffle-
joint, has neither sick-spleen, sleeping-evil, set-fast, or snaggle-
tooth, nor suppression of urine, sand-creaks, swelling-sheath,
subcutaneous sores, or shattered hoofs, is not sour, sulky, slow,
surly, stubborn, or sullen in temper, neither shy, sly, nor skittish, slow, sluggish, nor stupid. He never slips, slides, strays,
stalks, starts, stops, shakes, swells, snivels, snibbles, snuffles,
smarts, stumbles, or stocks in his stall or stable, and scarcely
or seldom sweats, has a showy, skittish switch tail or stern, and
a safe set of shoes to stride on. He can feed on stubbles, sheaf-
oats, straw, sedges, and Scotch grass, carries sixteen stones on
his stroke with surprising speed over a six-foot sod or stone
wall. His sire was the sly, sober Sydus on a sister of Spindle

> Shanks by Sampson and Sporter, son of Sparkler, who won the
> Sweepstake and Subscription Plate last season at Sligo. His
> selling price is sixty-six pounds sixteen shillings and sixpence
> sterling.
>
> — from a document advertising the sale of a horse,
> an early exercise in English by Owen Roe O'Sullivan

THE EVENING, after the drizzly day, has grown very lucent. The
sunset has left a celestial freshness with the world. It has turned
Scattery Island in Ballinskelligs Bay the hue of oxblood. The
mountains shimmer: the sharp light delineates the sheep, tiny
white particles, grazing on them.

Seán Murphy says this brilliance is deceptive: tomorrow will
likely be another bad day, "a spiritual day." But as he drives his
cattle to their lowland pastures, *sotto voce* he sings an Irish
poem composed by Owen Roe O'Sullivan, *Eoghan an Bheil
Bhinn*, Owen of the Sweet Mouth, and following the verse
(below, in my own translation],

> By cause of a woman came original sin;
> by cause of a woman's beauty Naisi fell;
> by cause of a woman flames lit Troy's towers;
> and by cause of a woman I'm in a smart mess.

he interjects, "There was a lot of family belonging to Owen
Roe." Then he finishes the song. Afterwards, he says, "I heard
that song from my mother. She couldn't read or write at all."

Seán is really in his element with Owen Roe. "Any song that I
would have belonging to Owen Roe, it can come very free in
me. There was lots of talent in Owen Roe, lots of great words; a
lot of good flattering speech, too. But the best of his poetry, it's
buried in the burying ground with him."

Owen Roe O'Sullivan can be taken as an Irish version of
Robert Burns, only he was less divided in his allegiances than
Burns was. A peasant poet, an itinerant potatoe-digger, he never
graced a literary tea with his presence. Poetry was what he did

between harvests. Not one of his poems saw print during his lifetime, and when they were at last taken from the lips of the Kerry country people by enterprising collectors, the *oeuvre* had blossomed wildly and it contained poems describing incidents that occurred after Owen Roe's death. In the oral public domain, they had become like living organisms, growing with the years and personal idiosyncrasy. The poet had become his admirers.

A scholarly outcry from these country people met the first edition of Owen Roe's poems, which appeared more than a hundred years after the poet's death. Some of them took credit for whole poems themselves, arguing that it was *their* poem appearing in *that* book, because they didn't like the idea of poems being printed in the first place — it must mean that poems were no longer adequate. Others would argue that a certain poem wasn't Owen Roe's at all, but the deathbed offering of a besotted beggar they had known *theirselves* in their youth, known only too well, a man who wasn't truly a poet at all but a perennial drinker and idler merely, never to be confused with the genius that was Owen Roe's. "That's not by Owen Roe. That was written by Mary O'Shea from Carriganimy beyond. I learned it for a wedding forty years ago. . . ." went one of the criticisms. The results of this edition, corrupt beyond repair, would have satisfied the poet.

The concept of Sweet Mouth compresses melodious words and kisses into a myth of flesh and poetry, inextricably bound. Today, the very old people are inclined to call Owen Roe, who died at thirty-six in 1784, the greatest poet who ever lived: this is as much for his procreative as for his creative abilities. Myriad are the anecdotes about him, and nearly all of them turn him into a totemistic figure, a fertility god of eighteenth century Munster. He was the bull who impregnated the Kerry cows. You can't throw a stone over a fence in Munster without bashing one of his descendants. He taught school to educate young women in the ancient art of fornication. Then, as a wandering tutor of Latin and Greek, he seduced the mothers of the children he was teaching, and the children, too. And so on.

The mountains where Owen Roe was born, *Da Chich Anann* ("The Tits of the Golden Dana"), are said to have given the poet an exalted suckling, from which he gained his legendary prowess. They resemble the full breasts of a reclining giantess, and the neolithic cairns at their peaks are her stark, erect nipples.

But, says Seán, disagreeing with this, "The gift came from Owen Roe's hair. There was something in his red hair that the women used to be mad after him. Then he had another gift: good, coaxing speech, he used to coax them. He said that the soft air is over the women all the time. All the young lassies and old women. Owen Roe was so popular, and he only a man five feet eight inches tall, or thereabouts." William Butler Yeats was — how tall? In the oral tradition, a respected personality, having once stood on substantial ground, remains capable of a certain human height which is no more trifling than one's own height. It proves he actually lived.

It amuses Seán to talk of Owen Roe's sexual exploits, and in Irish he has a perpetual store of these unpuritan stories. The deathbed stories, he thinks, are the most vigorous, and " 'Twould take a lifetime to tell them all." It amuses him, too, that many of them are contradictory.

"This lady wouldn't believe Owen was dead. She says, 'I'll soon know if Owen is dead.' She walked out and she went into the house that he was laid out, and she stood at his bed and pulled up her shift, and he didn't stir. She had it pulled up there for some time. 'You're dead,' she said. 'Twas then she found his last verses written on a scrap of paper:

> Weak indeed is the poet
> When the pen drops from his hand. . . .

"Now this is a little different story. Owen was a traveler, and I suppose this lassie did have contact with him before, and they wanted to know if he was on his way out, he was in this fever-hut in Knocknagree. So this twenty-year old said, 'I'll soon know.' She jumped into bed with him, and he — couldn't! That's when he made his last song, and there was nine twenties and nine with it. He had done that many women. That's when he says,

> Go, hag, and tempt me not with your old yellow cunt,
> A hundred and eight-nine young women I did set astray.

You see, he was explaining to her that he hadn't always been in the way of death."

It would be a delicate treachery, Seán thinks, to tell these stories in English; he suggests that if he did, they'd become somewhat tarnished and objectionable. He doesn't believe one should talk of sex, anyway, in English; he doesn't know why, he just says the Irish has more "talent" in it, that's what his father, who was a "scholar," had always said. To him, Irish cannot ever be translated into anything but itself. "Well, you know, when you say those things in English, the talent isn't in it. That's the only gift that was in the Irish, that there was great talent in it." But he soon modifies this blanket explanation for a more personal one. "The Irish, I suppose, is more in my blood."

In Owen Roe's time, to be a poet was no more a disgrace than to be a *spailpín* man, "a follower of the spade," which the poet was, wandering the relatively rich lands of Limerick and East Cork in search of harvests. Like poetry, it was not the most lucrative of professions. But when a man has little or no money, and little or no prospects for getting any, composing verses is scarcely different from not composing them. Seán recites a stanza from one poem (this time, he hasn't the air) which glosses the whole hard routine from the altitude of a man dedicated to his own dignity:

> 'Tis not poverty I hate the most
> Nor the eternal grovelling,
> But the insults which grow on it,
> Which not even leeches can cure.

"He was always naked poor," says Seán, with a sudden sharpness to his voice. "But 'tis lovely, them verses, anyways.

"Owen Roe used to give a good rubbing to the priests. He went to mass one day, and they were collecting at the gate — you would have to pay a penny, and he didn't have the penny, and the priest was at the door, and he was holding everybody out that wouldn't pay the penny. So Owen Roe walks in and he says, 'Oh I have no penny.' 'You'll go back,' the priest says. There was turf for the fire beside the church. 'Well,' Owen Roe said, 'if money is our religion,' he said, 'it isn't in the heavens no more, and I might as well sit down on that turf as to be listening to you reciting mass from the pulpit.' And he sat down on the turf."

In those penal days, however, the priests didn't object too much to these "rubbings," nor to the religious exhortations Owen Roe often mingled in his poems with panegyrics on the virtues of drink. Seán remarks that these priests had more pressing concerns: "The English hunted every priest we had — there was the same price on a priest's head as on a wolf's. The English did a lot of help to our religion. Anything you suppress, it becomes better.

"There was a priest named Father Fitzgerald at Owen Roe's death and he said that the loss of Owen Roe was greater than it would be if all the priests in Munster died of the plague, because priests can be created any day by reason of money, but all the money in Ireland at that time, it couldn't bring back a poet the likes of Owen Roe."

Then he pauses. Perhaps he has given the wrong impression. And he adds, "He was a grand Catholic, Owen Roe was." But this is not enough, it does little to capture the spirit of this scapegrace poet, so he says, "Oh yes, he was a pious, fornicating man."

There are white stockings in the burned heels today and the back of the hand given to the customs and manners of the old and alternative life being led. It can't be helped, I suppose, because life is changing as the years are passing along.

— Peig Sayers, *An Old Woman's Reflections*

"I used to always go to an old person for to get a few histories. 'Twas an old man that in 1928 told me this: he said that there was a wonderful man living just beyond here, a sheep herder for a Protestant landlord years ago, and this man had no knowledge of anything but his sheep and his lands. He was away up in the mountain beyond minding sheep, and he never seen a chapel, he was miles away from a chapel.

"There was a priest crossing one time, and the priest began to talk to this man, and he says, 'Do you go to mass?' 'What is that?' says he. The priest asked him his age, and he told him, a man well gone in years, a white bawneen he was wearing. 'Next Sunday,' says the priest, 'you'll see the people going to mass, and follow them. Follow them down the mountain.' 'All right,' says he.

"Sure enough, the next Sunday he followed them down the mountain and into the chapel. The day was very warm, and after walking, and when he was coming inside, he started to pour sweat. There was a sunbeam coming in from the window, and he thought it was a rope, and he took off his white bawneen and threw it up upon it, and faith, believe it or believe it not, the coat caught up on the sunbeam and the sunbeam kept the coat. Then the priest, seeing the coat hanging there, said to the congregation, 'Thanks be to God, there's a Saint at mass today.'

"After mass, the priest came up to the old man and told him he needn't come anymore. Why? Because he was a true Christian, a living Saint. Because if he continued coming to that chapel, could happen next Sunday, he could fall into sin and the sunbeam wouldn't hold up the coat. He might look at a handsome lassie, that's all the marks you need ever pass, that's a sin for you. So he stayed away for the rest of his life.

"You see, that man was an actual Saint. He was in the mountain all his life, out there on his own, and there was more religion in him than there could ever be if he went looking for it, at the chapel. I don't think the sunbeam would have held up that priest's coat.

"That happened for a fact. But they're very few Saints left in it today, of that you can be even more sure. No, not many Saints at all" — he chuckles — "and altogether too many priests, at least that's what I think. A good lot of them are in it for the money, turning the priesthood into a business. We have another saying around here: 'You'll never be rich til you have a son that's a priest.' There was a boy from here who left and went over to the States to be educated as a priest in such an order, and when they were nearly finished in their course and nearly ordained, this boy wrote to his mother: 'I'll be in this order all right, but from this time out, I won't be earning any money, because this order doesn't earn money.' The mother got up and flew to Chicago, to tell him if he wasn't going to make any money, sure, she wouldn't let him be a priest. Let him be a shopkeeper instead!

"At one time, a priest would beat you with his umbrella if he saw you going with a girl. If an unmarried lassie had a baby, the priest would go to the pulpit and cut the ground from there. Now today, 'tis just the opposite and just as peculiar, with the priests being matchmakers, trying to put the girls with the boys and the boys with the girls. Once, that bit of business was done by nature, now 'tis done by the priests. I think there must be another God here now."

Seán will go no farther than that. He does not lose himself in

worry over a world where the fickle priests outnumber the
Saints. I ask him if he really does believe that a man's coat could
be kept aloft by a sunbeam, and he shakes his head in the
negative, but then admits that "This one time it happened, anyway." The story itself has sanctified this incident, made it a
miracle, made it real for him. Stories allow for all kinds of
materializations; they are Seán's objects, and they are established in him like dolmens, thrusting out from the landscape of
his mind, testifying to forgotten certainties in a rapidly changing
world.

In truth, Seán is more critical of an overzealous Catholicism
than he is of casual atheism. He mentions a neighbor, a man
who is so tight, "he'd geld a louse and send the testicles to
market." These last years this man, a bachelor, has been seized
by a religious frenzy, and now he spends his time making faces
and fulminating against the pharisaical multitudes in Ballinskelligs. Most often, he tackles his enemies inside Sanderson's public
house. There, he trumpets his defiance, like a maddened elephant, careering against those of little faith. "He won't drink
more than a pint of an evening," says Seán. "But he needs that
little to get himself squarely on the side of God."

As for himself, Seán has never been promiscuous in matters of
faith. His own house is furnished with religious icons in nearly
every room, but they are traditional furnishings for such a
house, in such a place. They are as much a part of the house as
its foundation stones. One expects them to be there. And they
appear in this order as one walks through the house:

In the central sitting room, the mantelpiece has a statue of the
Blessed Virgin with wounds in each foot; the Sacred Heart,
diffusing peasant-gold rays; and Saint Patrick standing and
grasping the globe with one hand and blessing with the other.

Looming on the wall opposite the mantel like a medieval
altarpiece is a triptych featuring Pope John in the middle, being
the Father, and the Sacrificed Sons, John and Robert Kennedy,
flanking him on either side.

Above the kitchen stove is the Sacred Heart; next to the

kitchen door, an embroidered *Lead Me and Guide Me.*

The Sacred Heart, on the staircase, also above both beds in the two bedrooms upstairs. One bedroom contains a souvenir of a First Holy Communion and a postcard from the holy isle of Iona; the other bedroom contains a print where Christ gives communion to a child.

And in the upstairs corridor, the Immaculate Heart, pierced with a sword.

These reverential items provide the house with a tissue of decoration, which disavows its own worth, which says, if starkly and imperfectly, The spirit is superior to the Bathroom Beautiful. As for what remains in the rest of the house, it is distinguished by its complete absence of trumpery, by its refusal to admit those subtle little reminders of mortality, the sunset-sprayed landscape paintings, the umbrella stands, the potted plants, the scatter pillows, the bidets, the electric toothbrushes, the footstools, the thermostats, the Utrillos, the telephones, the Venetian blinds, the coffee tables, and the electronic gadgetry that somehow manage to comfort other people in their bereavement. In this house, however, there are clocks ticking noisily in every room.

From the outside, this two-storied dwelling is nearly Doric in its plainness. And seen from a distance, it has a modest gray grandeur and is all of a gray piece with the maze of stone walls around it, which have the traceried effect of hedges freaked with snow. Seán built this house himself out of stone he quarried from the bay thirty years ago. With a gesture of his hand, he identifies the place where he worked, and then he alludes to "the famous long bones of Ballinskelligs. They were in the monastery burying-ground down by the bay. We had a terrible storm a long time ago now, and some of the burying ground just fell off and dropped into the sea. Then you were able to see the long bones of monks — very large men — poking out the side of the cliff. For a long time, no fisherman would want to pass that spot by night, for fear he'd get some sort of curse placed on him or on his catch. For a few years, the people came from all over

Kerry to have a look at them. Well, those bones are all gone now. I think myself they just dropped into the sea."

Seán says he's like to give a *sénchas* now, a history, and he gestures that we should start walking back to the house. Had those moldering, vanished bones reminded him of it?

Of the qualifications of a Poet in Stories and in Deeds, here follows, to be related to kings and chiefs, viz.: Seven times fifty stories, i.e., Five times Fifty Prime Stories, and Twice Fifty Secondary Stories; and these Secondary Stories are not permitted (assigned) but to four grades only, viz., an *Ollamh*, an *Anrath*, a *Cli*, and a *Cano*. And these are the Prime Stories: Destructions, and Cattle-Raids, and Courtships, and Battles, and Caves, and Voyages, and Violent Deaths, and Feasts, and Sieges, and Adventures, and Elopements, and Slaughters.

— from the medieval *Book of Leinster*

". . . one night there were two men minding sheep in a valley, and they were saying the poems of the Fianna while they were there. And they saw two very tall shapes on the two hills on each side of the valley, and one of the tall shapes said to the other, 'Do you hear

that man down below? I was the second doorpost of
battle at Gabhra, and that man knows all about it better
than myself.' "
                — Lady Gregory, *Gods and Fighting Men*

It is not glossolalia. Seán does not go into a trance when he
narrates one of his histories. Quite the contrary. Clarity must
distill through his entire system for him to connect with the
arcane place in his memory where such things are lodged. Increasingly, he has to remind himself that such a place exists
before he is able to enter it; every three or four years, a folklorist
will "touch" him for a tale, and that is of some assistance in
activating his mind for the next folklorist. And he will give the
odd story to a summer class in Irish, practicing it beforehand
with his cattle. Beyond that, he is on his own, alone with his
memory, hoping only to keep out of the story what he calls
béarlachas, English words and constructions done over in Irish.

When someone tells him he might "improve" one of his tales,
Seán becomes adamant.

"It would spoil the history to add to it. With good Irish, you
could make up a story in your head, that's what they do in the
competitions. But in the histories about Finn McCool and
Cuchulainn and all those, there is no such thing as that you
could alter that, only by what you heard it. What happened
with Finn McCool, we could only tell that the way we heard it.
It would be the same as you saying something about President
Kennedy, that he went to war in the Crimean War instead of
the recent war.

"I could run two stories together if I wanted to and you
wouldn't know the difference, but I wouldn't do that no more
than I'd say mass. You see, I'd like to check and say, 'He's wrong
all over, there,' which I'd do, sure, if he's not telling the story the
way he heard it. And the same with myself, I'd like a person to
tell me I'm telling it wrong all over if I don't tell it the way I
heard it, and the way the man who told it to me heard it.

"It should be like a song, that the words fit together. I like to hear things the full way. Not in the way of the pictures [movies] that's going today — the ones today, he's here today and the next thing is, he's over in Africa. We don't see how he got out in Africa, what carried on in between. I once saw a make of picture, the beginning of it, and he's shot down, and in a matter of ten minutes, he's alive again and running. Now. Can you tell me why? Sure, I can't tell you."

With this sort of stringent assertion, Seán is speaking for the handful of shanachies left in the West. It is the rare man among them who'll admit to telling something different from the way he heard it, different from the way it was heard and recited years and years before them, back a tattered chiliad of Irish history; *they do no changing.*

And yet . . .

And yet, there is a license for everything, most of all poetic speech. These stories and histories *do* change with the telling, even on successive nights; their discrepancies are inspired by enthusiasm, testiness, languor, and the quantity of drink taken. The plot remains the same, along with the "runs," which are the shanachie's mnemonic tools. But many of the words and phrases in the narrative are created by the shanachie at the exact moment of telling; they have to do with personal abilities. Which is why Tomás Walsh could say that a man couldn't recite a wonder tale unless he was a "poet." It is a selfless tribute to the tradition out of which these narratives flow that so many "poets" claim they do no changing.

Seán views with some distaste the "competitions" he mentioned earlier. The most popular of these is the *Oireachtas*, a festival of Gaelic traditionality and chat originally devised by Douglas Hyde to rival the Welsh Eisteddfods and the Scottish mods. When the subject of the *Oireachtas* is broached, Seán can be counted upon to fix the broaching culprit with a stare that queries the man's moral fiber; to his mind, one might just as well bring up the subject of the relevence to Gaelic culture of the *Late, Late Show* on Irish television. Once, he participated in this cultural gala himself, traveling to Dingle or to Connemara where it was usually held. But this was before the slick commercial performers, panting after the trophies, appeared on the scene. Especially, he inveighs against the storytellers who made their reputations at the *Oireachtas* by memorizing their stories, mulling them over and over again, from printed texts.

"Some of those shanachies, they have only two stories, and them from a book, and then they go ahead and win the *Oireachtas*. The stuff that's coming from those men, it's coming through education. Then they give it off like they was on the *Late, Late Show*, they do. That is no good. The adjudicators should give credit to the shanachie who have Irish from the cradle, that's the proper Irish. You can tell my stories aren't book stories."

Nor is Seán sure he knows why storytellers and musicians must compete with one another in the first place.

"I will tell a piece about Conan Maol, Bald Conan, the bitter one of Finn McCool's men," says Seán. "A great, nasty man, that had on his backside a black sheep's fleece all his life, instead of the skin of a man. It was this way with him":

> Conan's life among the demons —
> If bad for him, for them no better.

Seán's wife, who has been listening quietly to him, excuses herself and goes into the kitchen. Seán says she isn't interested in stories; can't comprehend the Irish that's in the stories, anyway. In the old days, too, women were supposed to absent themselves from these felicities, which were fraught to the saturation point with male biases and male heroics; it wasn't right for the person who did the wash to hear the measured rhythms of the wonder tale. However, Seán remarks that she just isn't interested, never was, and besides, he'll need a cup of tea to moisten his throat after he tells this tale about Conan Maol.

One of his sons, who has also been listening, leaves for a nocturnal football match.

Before beginning, however, Seán again insists that he's not going to be telling a detached piece of fiction, but an event integral to the history of the race, and that is why there'll be no contrived "beginning" or "ending." He will begin in the thick of things, and the conclusion of the story will be the possible start of another story, "that's the way it is with history."

"My old story starts here . . ."

And he begins to work his elbows and knees like a fiddler, synchronizing the Irish word-rhythms to these terse physical movements. He chants it in the same hieratic way Yeats read his own poetry: gravely, dispassionately, almost as though it had died en route while straining his lips for release. A devotee of the theater might say that such an ascetic performance can only serve to keep people away. No sweeping gestures inform the listener what and when to feel. Nor does Seán trade in the suspenseful buildup or the pregnant pause ("People would think that if you'd pause, you'd be making it all up"). The stately cadences of his speech are all there is, and a few phrases singled out here and there and stressed above the rest for their native richness. It is not the events but the words peddling them that appear to matter most to him: *they* are heroic. The whole experience of listening to him prohibits a facile response, which may be one of the reasons the shanachie's audience has abandoned him for the *Late, Late Show*.

". . . Finn and the Fianna were using up food and drink together when a giant dressed in the skins of a wild beast walked in on them without passing a blessing on them. This giant had thick legs and thick hair, matted and crawling with worms, and he spoke in a fierce, rough voice. Bald Conan rose up, always a big, bold fellow without any sense, and when he rose up, he scattered the chessmen on the grass. Conan hit the giant on his jawbone, then Finn himself rose and put the blame on Conan because he hit a stranger without any reason or excuse. Conan said, 'A nice sweet blessing from a visitor is like a breeze blowing in from the harbor, but when a man comes in to our midst without passing a blessing on us, how do we know he's not an animal without sense? And there's nothing to be done with him but to lay a fist on his jawbone.' The giant said, 'I was sent on a message from the Viking side, to give an invitation to the Fianna to use up food and drink with the king of that country. But I would like to put a little word of advice in your ear, Finn McCool, High King of Ireland, that you don't take as your spear of protection anything but an old food knife, because the worst enemy that Finn McCool ever had was a big mouthful of words.'

"And then the Fianna leaped up, and prepared themselves against the wide sea, and made ready to leave Bald Conan behind as a punishment for his hasty fist. And Bald Conan came to Finn, and said, 'May the blessings of God be on ye, High King of Ireland, King of all the Fianna, descendant of the Milesians of Spain. I hope you will let me join your group of men.' Finn said, 'I'll give you a galleon of gold if you'd just go home and keep the women company!' 'Thank you very much, Finn McCool!' Conan said, 'but when you were a baby, you spent several hundred years yourself lying on your stomach in the ashes of the fire, with a wolf's bone in your mouth, until coolness baptized you, little-man Finn. So I lay this on ye: That you may be seven hundred times worse this time next year, if you are the king, little-man Finn.' That was a terrible curse to put on him, that Conan offered.

"Finn launched his fleet of boats with his own shoe, and sent it out swimming. The kick was strong enough to raise aloft the great-shining, firm-cordaged sails to the tops of the trees that were their masts. Then Finn and all the Fianna grasped their broad-bladed, well-made oars, and sailed out to sea in their towering, wide-wombed, broad-sailed vessels, and left Conan behind on the strand. And they went further and further, past the Isle of Mannanan MacLir and past all Scotland, riling up the water so that the smooth sand went to the bottom and the rough sand came to the top, and so that the small eels knotted themselves up with the big eels. Finn and his crew ploughed up the wild lonely sea in this fashion making their journey towards Viking country.

"Then it was that Bald Conan went to Mannanan MacLir, and said, 'The blessings of God upon ye, I hope you will let me follow that boat to Viking country.' Well, Mannanan said, 'I will put magic on your shadow, in such a way that they will see neither yourself nor your curragh. You'll be three days and three nights before you reach Viking country.'

"And so, the Fianna went on ploughing up the wild lonely sea, and Bald Conan went on as well, and they saw neither himself nor his boat because of the magic put on his shadow, and after three days and three nights, he came up to the big navy of the Fianna, and he put his head out, and called up to Goll McMorna, saying, 'Goll brother, I wonder which is the hardest, the board of your ship or the wood on the top of your head.' Goll did nothing except to push his hand out and try to hit Conan, but he couldn't see him.

"Conan continued on, anyway, until he came on to Viking country. When he landed, the king of the Vikings didn't recognize him, because he had been helped by Mannanan to the garb and sword of the Red Lances, that were killed in Ireland by Finn and the Fianna. When the guard let him in, he saw the king's mother, and she of a very ancient age and put in a cradle hanging over the door of the house. When she saw Conan, she was very alert, even though she was of an ancient age and put in a cradle. She said, 'I recognize the garb and sword of the Red Lances on ye, but I don't recognize the likeness or the person himself.'' Conan hadn't left the strand without putting a stone shaped by the sea in his wallet. He put his hand in his wallet, and took out the stone, and threw it at her, and he gave her a hit on the forehead which killed her. The Viking king came in when he heard his mother was dead, and said, 'You're a very touchy person to kill my mother.' Conan said, 'She went into a talking that drew great blame upon herself, and it is said that old women should always keep their mouths shut. So, sleep now, old woman.' The king said, 'It is well, then.' And Conan said, 'I have heard you asked Finn McCool to come over from Ireland, that you may murder him, and I am here to help you. But first I hope you will lend me a bride till morning.' 'I will give you my daughter till morning,' said the king. When they were put in the castle in bed, the king's daughter told Conan how Finn and the Fianna were to be deceived: two Vikings would stand on each side of them at the feast, and they the roughest, largest, most stout men in all the Viking lands.

"The next morning, Conan left his bride and went to the king, who said, 'Come with me, and we'll walk down to a cave to Tuathal, my son. I'm feeding him with beef marrow and chicken broth, so he can pull down the strength of Finn McCool who's coming from Ireland.' 'It is well, then,' said Conan. They went down to the cave, and the son was there, a big hero of a lad. See here in this man all the things which appertain to the character of the hero!

"Tuathal saw Conan, and took him to be Darrig, who was the king's cousin. He put a hundred thousand welcomes before the Big Red One, Conan. 'Sit down,' Conan said, 'and we'll have a game of cards.' They sat down, and they went at playing cards. Tuathal won the first game, so Conan told him, 'Pass your judgment.' 'Ah, musha,' Tuathal said, 'I ask you to lay your head on this stone block, and I'll pull out my battle-ax, but I won't draw it down on ye.' 'It is well,' said Conan. He lay back, and put his head on the block. Tuathal brought down the ax to a bird's feather of Conan's neck, but he didn't harm him with it. Conan got up, and they went at playing a second game of cards, and Conan won. Then Tuathal said, 'Pass your judgment now.' 'I will,' said Conan, 'so put your head down nicely on the stone block, and when I swing my battle-ax above your neck, don't let fly with a scream or whistle.' So Tuathal put his head tastily back on the block, and Conan swung his battle-ax, and took his head clean off. 'Ah,' Conan said, 'He who goes by the sword must expect to die shamelessly by it!' So Tuathal died unknown to his country by Conan's giant battle-ax.

"Then it was that the fleet of boats of Finn McCool landed on the strand, and Bald Conan was before them, and when he met them, he said, 'A hundred thousand welcomes to ye, Finn Mc-Cool, High King of Ireland.' 'It can't be that you are Bald Conan,' said Finn. Conan said, 'I am that same man, and you've been given a false invitation by the Viking king, and it would be well for ye to be very careful.' Said Finn, 'Go off, you are only a Red Lance knight trying to vex us. Bald Conan we left across in Ireland.' Said Goll McMorna, 'You aren't Conan, because Conan I made to drown when he came alongside my boat in the middle of the wild lonely sea.' 'Ah, Goll,' said Conan, 'You must sharpen the blade of your knife at both ends, and hide it on yourself under the flesh of your arm, for you will be searched when you enter the king's castle.' Then Conan showed them his bald head, and soon the Fianna knew who this great, nasty fellow was.

"And so Finn and the Fianna went up to the king's castle, and they were well armed against a false invitation. The king of the Vikings put a hundred thousand welcomes before them, and he led them to the table, but before they sat down, all their battle-axes and dirks were taken from them. When they were in at the table using up food and drink, Finn looked behind him — and there wasn't a man of the Fianna present who didn't have two rough, large, stout Norse giants standing behind him. Finn said, 'I have to put my thumb in my mouth, and chew it to the marrow, because now I am sure it is a false invitation we have gotten.' Then Finn put his thumb in his mouth, and chewed it to the marrow, and he said to all the Fianna, 'We have gotten a false invitation and the men behind us are going to take off our heads!' And then he said to Conan, 'Oh Bald Conan, are you able to do anything for us?' 'Oh, I am,' said Conan. 'Eat away!'

"Then Bald Conan went to Mannanan MacLir again, and Mannanan put a powerful bill the size of a bee's stinger on him, and he put wings on the big Bald One's back. Then Conan flew back to the Viking land, and he began the fight by poking out the eyes of the Vikings who were outside the feast and those who were in the kitchen as well. He did this until word was carried to the king about it, that unless this devilish fellow was stopped, there wouldn't be a single eye in a single head of any Viking in all the Viking land. 'I will not let my battle-ax down until that fellow is turned away,' said the king. The king raised his battle-ax higher than an oak tree above Conan's head, but the big Bald One with his bill took off the king of the Viking's head and then kicked it into the sea. Then he took the king's daughter, and he ground her body to pieces in a mill that was made for trees.

"And so Finn said to Conan, 'You have cut the first flesh, and we must now go into battle because we have gotten a false invitation.' Then the High King of Ireland, the king of all the Fianna, Finn McCool, pushed through the Vikings like a hawk through a flock of birds. And they won, the Fianna won the battle."

Seán nods his head very slightly to indicate he has finished. His wife brings out the tea.

"The man I got that history from is dead with forty years, and he was about eighty-four at the time I took it from him."

But for now, Seán would prefer to escape to the present; his mind has been fairly sapped of its remembering powers by the concentration Conan Maol drew forth from it.

"I maintain that President Kennedy gave too much liberty to the darkies," he says, sipping at his tea.

When I disagree with this, he replies: "Well, I believe we should let every herring hang by its own tail." This is a very old proverb, and he utters it in mellifluous Irish. For he is, in the root sense, a deeply cultivated man.

My Father Was a Great Man
at the Harvesting

Progress is the injustice each generation commits with regard
to its predecessor.

— E. M. Cioran

Is it the same place?" said Mary, sadly, as she looked down
the hill. There was a low stone wall at each side of the road, the
mortar of which looked very new and unpleasant to the eye.
Perhaps the mortar looked all the more fresh because of the
dark stones that seemed to thrust themselves through it here
and there, in order that the traveller might read the story of
quenched hearths and scattered households in their soot-
browned faces. An odd tree, a perch or two in from the road,
marked the boundary of a "haggart;" for where an ash or an
elm sheltered the peasant's cabin the tree was allowed to stand.
The beech-tree escaped in this way; and the pointed gable of
Phil Lahy's old house, now roofless and crumbling to decay,
seemed to regard the change wrought by the rule of the
Stranger with a grim smile. . . . No smiling faces now as they
went on; no children's voices; no ringing of the anvil. . . .

"It is an awful change," Mary observed.

"It really is," returned Grace. "I thought of it when you
said we would go through *the village.*

— Charles J. Kickham, *Knocknagow*

AN OPEN VIEW of the landscape around Seán Murphy's house
takes in many other dwellings, as well as outbuildings which
were formerly dwelling places themselves; a continuous peb-

bling of structures on the boreens that writhe up and around this mountainy land. Like many other infertile regions in the West, the peninsula of Iveragh was so thick with people at the end of the last century, it was called a "Congested District," which made it eligible for grants, fisheries, and savings banks. Holdings were redistributed; suddenly, small farmers found themselves with actual acreages of land; and new houses were constructed in what is sometimes labeled the "Congested Districts" style — a three-room, rectangular, single-level selflessness usually perched on or near a rise. Many of the houses around Seán are of this style. In the West, they are still said to be "new," perhaps because like other new things, like motorcars, they sacrificed health for expediency. All too often, atop their hillocks, they were exposed to ceaseless gusts of wind. The older, clustered houses had been built out of the way of the weather.

"Black '47," the Great Famine, helped relieve some of this congestion, thinning numbers through starvation or America. But the Famine also herded people from the interior of Kerry to its seacoast, Seán's locale, in search of the periwinkle and dogfish, meats they had not known previously; famine or its agent, the English, had earlier forced them westward from their plundered lands east of the River Shannon, which contains the richest soil in Europe between the Atlantic Ocean and the Ukraine.

West. It was always west they went. There, at least, famine could make them strong willed, and make them resourceful in the most elemental ways. Beside *that* fact, certain upstart economic programs seem right now to the small farmer as the palest of gossamers dangling in an Atlantic gale, and devious as only words coffined on paper can be: the Farm Retirement Scheme, the Small Farmer Incentive Scheme, and the Farm Modernization Scheme. These are just more "scheming" from a government now dedicated to the survival of the biggest, whatever it may be, the biggest farms, the best foreign investments, the biggest of common markets. And done up in a heavily latinated, clogged English, the pamphlets on these various schemes seem literally to resemble eviction notices more than anything else. A person couldn't begin to understand an eviction notice, either. The lesson of Irish history is that any footsteps other than a man's own may trample him, and an Incentive Scheme is an alien footstep, marching quickly and forcefully onward; the wild risk of availing one's self of the scheme's credit touches bad racial memories. What would happen if one could not pay back the rather large debt implied in this credit operation? The county workhouse is gone, but recollection of it lingers on.

The small farmers who own televisions can always watch programs that inform them of up-to-date agricultural methods. However, these programs, like the larger governmental programs, focus on commercial holdings to the detriment of the low-income farm and its problems. And to the man of little means, watching his bit of furniture (as Seán Murphy might say), the matter of farm modernization lives in the same exotic realm as an American gangster film. The television couples modernity and gangsters together in a dance of fantasy: they hug each other on the same bed. No gangster is likely to appear in Ballinskelligs with a blackjack, nor is the small farmer there likely to change from the old ways. These are fantastical things, like a burnoosed Berber. No — even on his televised rock, the Berber commands a greater actuality.

The reluctance to innovate has created a race of survivors in the West: a lifeboat cresting the waves of a body of water that has dried up. Except for this reluctance, there might not be any life here at all. Conservative farming practices save resources better than those derelict resources deserve. And the yield of the traditional small farm is low only in the short-term view; in a man's life, it is enough. A single season is a very short time in the West, where land is often measured by the number of lifetimes embraced by it. "I can go back a long ways," a man in his eighties said to me as he rested from scything hay in his Galway field. But compared to this field, he was still quite young.

February, a few days after Saint Brigid's Day. A flannel sheet of clouds hangs over the mountains, which pose in the distance like idols in a joss house. An abrupt blessing of warm air gives promise of the dry days of spring ahead, when there'll be turf to cut, manuring, hoeing, perhaps even the sale of a cow or two.

I have come to the small Connemara village of Carna because I've heard Tadhg Sugrue, a small farmer living just outside the village, tell stories on Radio na Gaeltachta, the Irish language radio station of the West. I find Tadhg in the process of digging his garden for potatoes, and I ask him if I can be of assistance, since I hope to barter a few hours' labor for a story. But there is just enough ambiguity in my broken Irish for Tadhg to confuse me with Tom O'Donnell, the minister for the Gaeltacht. It appears that he was expecting a reply at about this time from the minister, to whom he had written concerning his fourteen-year-old "simple" daughter; the past year, his family hadn't received the full stipend alloted to native speakers on account of this girl, who isn't able to speak properly in any language. When the local adjudicator in all his strictness came to check on the Irish, he took her poor babbling to be a closer approximation of English than Irish, which it wasn't, "It wasn't anything." I apologize; I tell him that, under the circumstances, I *should* have been Tom O'Donnell. At which he himself apologizes. Though he doesn't know Mr. O'Donnell from Adam, he says he would take it as an insult to be mistaken for a government minister, "with the way the West is going, falling downhill, downhill all the way."

Tadhg walks back to the vegetable garden with a slight hitching of his right shoulder, the result, he tells me, of an accident he incurred several years ago when he fell from his donkey, which he had mounted at the request of a Dublin visitor who had wanted to photograph him on the animal, "for old time's sake." But even that injury now seems part of the casual rhythm his body makes in conjunction with the stoniness he calls his property; the land in this section of Connemara makes even Seán Murphy's part of Kerry seem like the Good Earth.

I watch Tadhg move the soil with his spade. It may be the "fall" of the world, his world, but through this activity, taken in itself, his clay manages to escape the implacable weight of its destiny: he just digs and digs. His style of turning the land includes four hundred years of these Februarys. Tradition has it that Sir Walter Raleigh introduced the potato into Ireland in 1588 to provide more subsistence than grain on small plots of land, as Tadhg's is still. But Sir Walter — I mention the name to Tadhg because it is appropriate to the job at hand — he has never heard of. He does, however, know the names of all the families in his area who suffered greatly during the potato famine. "There, across that field, they were Corbetts. The husband died first, and the woman still used to go out every day with a basket on her back to see could she get a few potatoes. But this day she came back, and the basket was empty, and there was a little girl belonging to her, she was running up the road agin her, and the woman lay down the basket and when the little girl looked into the basket and nothing in it, she fell dead. Ah, my grandmother told me that. She remembered the night of the big wind, and she brought me to a place outside Roundstone, and she showed me seven graves of people she knew right well." There, in his grandmother, is his relation to the Famine: a blood relation.

Where he says the Corbetts lived, there is now only the waste of heather, spattered with various sizes of rock that look like generations of rock growth, boulders, mere stones, crumbled stones, whole families of pebbles. This is the heraldry of Connemara, together with the gutted shells of houses, the gouged eyesockets of their windows staring at the road. A famine thought: this region has lost more people these last ten years through emigration than it lost during the entire potato blight. And they continue to leave, even still, preferring low-skill jobs in Dublin, Glasgow, and Birmingham to low-skill jobs in any of the several industries recently put in the Gaeltacht in one last attempt to save people for this most native of places. So it is a matter of tradition rather than of available work — birds fly away from the home nest at a certain age because they've developed the wings to do just that. And it is also an intense yearning to escape this solitude of stone, which was once a way of life in itself.

Tadhg's own land is a tract of stone and pasturage squeezed into eighteen acres. It achieved this handkerchief size long ago through division among sons and the sons of sons, through countless antique generations of Sugrues. Such partitioning of land was the consequence of the old penal laws, which prevented a Catholic from leaving all his land to one son. Tadhg's one son Liam — he has five daughters, but that means nothing in terms of a life based on patrilineal succession — has already accepted his inheritance from his father, determined as he is to wrench a profit from this stingy land for the first time. Instead of farming it, however, Liam has isolated two acres for a bed and breakfast establishment. In fact, the new guest house is already nearing completion. Liam, a clerk in a Dublin shoe store, has been driving down on weekends for nearly a year now to do work on it.

Tadhg points to the new building with a degree of pride. After all, his son made it. Yet he hardly needs to point to it, for it dwarfs his own modest cabin, directly in front of which it has been constructed, like a dinosaur placed alongside the first man. The new house, a two-floor bungalow with a tile roof, somewhat resembles a glassed-over army barracks. What it sacrifices in the way of harmony with the landscape, it will bring back with crowds of tourists. There will be plenty of people here once again. Once again congestion, yet this time at the expense of history: under the foot of the tourist, all custom is trampled, as the grass must surely have been trampled under the hoofs of Attila the Hun's horses.

"It is all shoes with Liam, you know," Tadhg observes. The barest trace of a frown on his face perhaps suggests that, being a man enmeshed with the land totality of his life, he can't quite understand why anyone would want to spend his time selling shoes. When I ask him what he thinks of his son's decision to court holiday-makers in his own front yard, he just smiles and says, with something akin to approval, "It'll be soft money."

With this last insight, Tadhg forces his spade into the ground to expose the rust-colored loam with a little more energy than before. Guests may lurk just over the horizon, yet it is still all handwork with him. Not the shoework demanded by the pedals of a tractor. Small farmers like him are usually unable to afford the luxury of big machines, and even if they could, in country like Tadhg's the recalcitrant ground would not tolerate that sort of object. A man's drumlins must be hand ploughed. But around here, Tadhg says, there were once enough men of a single family to do the work of machines. "In my father's time, there was himself and my six brothers, and we were proud to be able to say we did all the work ourselves. Would they go into debt with the Irish government trying to keep up the land? Not at all! We'd sooner give it up altogether — join with Duffy's circus instead of getting ourselves great with debts and those things." Like Seán Murphy, he doesn't feel that any of the various government schemes lend themselves to personal liberty. His solution: just to continue on, and hope that his hands last him six more years, when he'll be eligible for the old-age pension.

I glance at those crucial hands. They look like the roots of trees, all gnarled and knotted. The freckles on them, like the blotchings on a trout, show that he had once been fair. "My father was a great man at the harvesting," Tadhg says suddenly, in Irish.

Then I notice the tall mast of an aerial rising from the slate roof of his cabin. A television? I ask. Yes, he says, a gift from

Liam. A comfort in the winter. Then perhaps he watches some of the farming programs presented weekly on this "comfort"? He hedges a little. He is a bit ashamed. But yes, he does watch them, the only problem being that he really doesn't have the English to follow them very well, the people speak too fast, slur their words, and he can only get scraps here and there, "just foreign words to me, and no doubt those farming shows would be useful if they was in Irish, too." Yet he even prefers to divulge his insecurity with English in English, despite the fact that his Irish is, a Connemara neighbor says, "better than his own father's."

His predicament, I think, may be something like this. The television, whenever he turns it on, chides him for speaking the wrong language, tells him he's rather retarded for speaking the language of the legendary oppressed, when all the action lies elsewhere. The latest uprising in Timor, say, is staged in English, for the benefit of the native English speaker. In English, there is the drug problem, the cod war, the Common Market, crime in the streets, teenage sex, the Loch Ness monster, Generalissimo Franco's death, homosexuality, and other news of contemporary interest. "News," by definition, is still alive, continuing to happen; it is the current rage in Timor or the world of fashion. Tadhg appears to realize that the bland goat-faces on his television screen are often less interesting than certain stones in the path of his plough. But even that makes him the odd man out until there is a television series dedicated to the life stories of stones. So he can't help but feel like a curio as he sits in front of this machine, which gives him the whole world with a single button, gently pushed; and I doubt if he can help wondering why it is people like himself are so often the butts of video ridicule, such as the recent variety program that promised an interview with a small Galway farmer and then showed its interviewer talking to a midget in overalls. Perhaps if a fellow watched the *Wodehouse Playhouse*, he could learn what to say.

"Backward," that word keeps surfacing in Tadhg's talk. He wants me, an outsider, to know that he is not backward. Just because he lives in the wilds of Connemara doesn't mean he is a wild man. He knows a modicum of English, see. Finally, he lets the donkey out of the byre (as it were): "There was a radio man living here this past year, and he'd go on Dublin radio twice a week with a different tale on the people living here, myself too. He made us out to be right fools, that fellow! One time he said he met me at the well drawing my water and two hours we talked about the weather, standing there. Well, that day we did meet, and we didn't talk more than fifteen minutes, because I knew your man and I was trying to escape him. I knew he'd pull a trick like that one on me. And then he went on once about the men of this place wearing hobnail boots everywhere, in the fields, everywhere. Can you imagine?"

In fact, I don't need to imagine. When a few minutes later I happen to notice Tadhg's boots, I discover that he is wearing — the hobnail variety. It is the dread backwardness, silently and snugly there all along. Of course, I could prod him with this apparent contradiction, but there'd be no point in taunting this man, who is in full control of his country senses, as though he were a withered, tea-towel personality. Is he, a storyteller, trying to drive me off the foot-scent of my prey with a lie? I decide that it isn't a lie — in Carna. In the land around this village, there are two entirely different makes of hobnail boots. There is the type Tadhg wears, purchased at a time when the roads were softer, and there is the boot espoused by the radio, fitted for public consumption, a media boot offered as the quaint foot piece of a quaint folk.

All I can say on my own behalf, having just opened myself up to this same criticism by observing these boots on him, is that I find very little quaintness in Tadhg. He would not know what stage gestures to make in a Barry Fitzgerald film, nor what to say in a drinking bout with Brendan Behan. Indeed, it is the survival powers, the lasting in the hobnail boot that is so remarkable. This plain, insignificant object comes out of a culture that also had that last in it; beside that culture, Brendan Behan, his stomach bloated with drink, is a thin figure. Now, however, it is nearly over; the few remaining blacksmiths no longer put metal plates on these boots. And the former strengths of the culture itself have become weaknesses in many eyes. Perhaps too many jokes have been made in public. Perhaps too few men have been sold on Incentive Schemes. Perhaps there have been too many people with too little money. The last days of a culture are full of perhapses. But one thing is certain: before long, to articulate thought in the old terms will be as absurd as the case of the Irish missionary-priest who, having just arrived in Nigeria, began to lecture a group of half-naked tribesmen on the grave dangers of dancing at the crossroads.

OBITUARY NOTICE

The death took place during the week of Anthony Curran of Galway Road, Clifden. One of the last surviving town criers in Ireland, the late Mr. Curran was well-known in Clifden and the surrounding countryside.

When his remains were being removed from St. Joseph's Church to Ardbeare Cemetery for burial, the people of the town carried his coffin on the route as a final tribute to one who had carried many announcements and public messages through the same streets over his megaphone down through the years.

— *Connaught Tribune*, November 28, 1975

Once a month, Tadhg puts on his suit of Donegal tweed (whose wool, however, comes from Australia) and a local schoolmaster drives him to the town of Spiddal, where he delivers a story over the Connemara branch of Radio na Gaeltachta.

Sometimes, it'll be a comic fable; sometimes, if the right mood strikes him, it'll be an old wonder tale. He seldom knows beforehand what story will escape his lips, and he never practices a story in advance, saying that "the story is there in your head anyway, whether you practice it or whether you don't." Whichever story he chooses to tell from behind the microphone, his honorarium remains the same: five pounds.

"You ask me would I tell the stories if I wasn't paid for them. Well, I don't think I would. I'll give you the root of the tree now. I have seen my countrymen suffer" — the English words, which he insists on using with me, aren't coming out here in the order he wants them, and he catches himself up, revamping the sentence — "My countrymen suffered terrible for hundreds of years, no hope, no ray of sunlight coming to live on their face. We went through all those years, and the only thing going was stories, which we told to pass the night. That was all. When I was a lad, I sat at the feet of a great storyteller here named Folan, and 'twas near rags he'd be wearing, 'twas. I'd be as full of that as I'd be of his stories, the listening of them.

"For years and years, so, there never was money in stories, and that was right. The like of stories should be apart from money, but the way it catches my eyes now, I'm getting a bit back on the time when we had nothing but our stories to live by.

"Ah well, maybe I would tell them for free, like."

Perhaps Tadhg is getting "a bit back" on the radio itself, which had embalmed him at the well with a bucket of water, by forcing it to yield to his stories. Mating himself with the media, he can now be heard as far afield as Donegal, though scarcely understood there, where the local dialect is closer to Scottish Gaelic than it is to Connemara Irish. At home, though, a number of people who would never think of dropping in on him for a story do tune in to him on the radio. It only takes a simple twitching of the fingers. One of his neighbors, the woman living next door to him, says: "I listen to Tadhg well enough. Aye, he is nice enough to hear. It'd remind you of the old days. But them things are forgotten now, well forgotten." To reverse the old adage, Forgotten but not yet gone; forgotten, and Tadhg caught with them on him still. Every four weeks, the radio replaces him with — himself, a ghost, an unfleshed version of his former self. He has become like the stomach, which continues to digest even after death; so, too, has he survived his own oblivion. A radio star? Not even that, for not enough people are able to understand what he's telling them. Yet he is well pleased; it is not at all backward to tell a wonder tale in Irish on Radio na Gaeltachta.

To get a story, a man once needed to walk. As a young man, Tadhg walked four miles nearly every night to hear the "greatest" of the local shanachies; he mentions this distance as casually as if it were just out back. When he was older, he got his stories within the confines of his own house, from the unexpected source of his own father: "My mother was buried the past forty years. There was no one with me, only the old man, my father, and he had stories in Irish, songs in Irish. He was sick with pleurisy and everything else, and I stayed inside with him eight or nine years every night. I did not leave him inside any night until he died, and I was thankful for that; he wouldn't like to go to tablets at all. No, he ordered to die alongside the fence outside the house. I didn't even have a doctor or nurse for him, and he was ninety years. I won't, says I. When I give the inch, I give the foot. For eight years, so, I picked Irish stories out of his head. Until that time, I hardly ever looked to him for stories. I didn't know he had them on him. But when a man is dying, they say all the life on the inside comes out, there you can touch it."

Eight years with a dying man, hearing stories — that would seem to support him in his toughness, darkening him with his own mortality. But his soft round face, rising from a long neck wrinkled like a vulture's, contains barely a hint of the anguish-chiseled features of the literary peasant. I watch this face, waiting for it to break open with some abrupt expression giving flesh to eight years of unhappiness. And he just spits, in a philosophic way. Not at me or at the world, but at the contemptible ground his companion. Then it strikes me: if some people derive their features from the look of where they live, others can take on the feelings of their geography, and Tadhg has become Connemara, inside. After a fashion, he is growing bereft of people.

I wonder when it was Tadhg last told a story — in person. Twenty years ago, he says, twenty years ago he told them to his son, "and he liked them, a lad. I don't expect he could understand them, but he liked them. When he got so he could understand them, he'd blast them out of the house! Around here now, the people believes that the stories are too . . . ancient . . . and homely and it'd be best not to tell them while they're trying to get their children to bigger places where they'd be better off. And they are a wee simple, those old stories, aren't they?" Casually, he scans my face for my reaction. He is sounding me out, trying to make certain that my questions aren't designed to make a mockery out of him. I tell him that I think these stories are no more simple than the way of life from which they are inseparable, explaining it, redeeming it. To which he responds, with little levity in his voice, "Yes, they were great entertainment, right enough."

My education should have taught me a method of placing a hesitant shanachie at his ease, rather than offering me the spectacle of photosynthesis, which would still occur even if I never knew about it. Early on, I should have been told the truth, that human life is far more fragile than plant life, despite the illusory stems, flowers, and petals — strong, versatile, resilient things compared to the fibers of human trust. For a man alive and at the end of his words, like Tadhg, is more valuable than all the dead substance dosed out by teachers as though their students also enjoyed carrion. There are lessons to be learned from the end of the world.

"I only tell stories on the radio now," says Tadhg. "It is only on the radio I'm well able to tell a story."

We take our rest on the ground near a sheep's skull with a

scraggly, disused jackdaw's nest in it. A harmony of hollowness, I think, lacking only an empty egg in the nest to fulfill its negative promise.

Fat, fleecy clouds begin to materialize out of the naked blue sky with that suddenness one often finds when a place seems to have the ability to make its own weather. One of these clouds so resembles the shape of Ireland that I point it out to Tadhg. "'Tis like the map of Africa, that one," he says, pointing to another. And as we switch from clouds to the affairs of the world, it becomes increasingly obvious that he will not tell a story. He wants me to respect him as a citizen of the world, a place he does not equate with stories, and although I try to indicate that I'd respect him more for being a citizen of Carna, a much more sane and civilized place, it is no use. An attack of newsiness overtakes him, and he asks me in quick succession what I think of Princess Grace and General Amin (as if together they comprised a vaudeville act), and whether I'd agree with him, that Ireland would be in a more salvageable state today if Conor Cruise O'Brien, the present Minister of Posts and Telegraphs, had been lost in the Congo years ago. But before I can respond to any of these queries, he observes that "the flow of communism throughout the world is going to be a very difficult thing to stop." This last sentence is delivered in faultless English, and seems to have come to him from somewhere outside the Gaeltacht. But he does look somewhat worried.

I am tolerant of this fear of Tadhg's. It is a dream of death by drowning, a flow of vast waters over him, terrible in their impersonal grayness. It portends the loss of life through the loss of identity, and an endless high tide at Carna.

Note on the decline of communism in the west of Ireland:

The land around a man must be fathomable, and a world community is much too large to fathom, except in the general realization that it is all-engulfing. It is only in a small and intimate world, one which is comprehensible in human terms, that the essential features of life — work, play, the growing of food — can connect with each other directly. In the loss of that small world exists the true dying of the West. Rocks where people had once been. Pasturage replacing the old neighborhoods. More and more landless workers, city men, men without a country. Unemployment problems, for the first time. Entertainment growing indistinguishable from big business. And the rural remnants informed that they must now compete with each other in order to survive the deadly game of farming.

The small communities of the West were collectives in their own fashion. Mutual aid insured that a man had help with his farm work, especially if his own family was small. And if a man had surplus produce, it would be shared among the people around him. There was no competition because there was no way of making the land profitable. A turnip cannot be bled, only eaten.

In this same infinitely small world, stories brought people who had given each other aid together again in a commune of listening. A night of storytelling was like a putting into words of the day's work, making it comprehensible and also heroic, if that night a hero tale was told. Rather as though it were a continuation and not just a reward for all that contact with living and growing things. It was like the harvest itself. The fictional setting of these stories may have been ancient Ireland, but the real setting was the openly human one by the hearth, a full embrace of fire, language, and seated company. By contrast, television is a necessarily private vice.

"It was not the story that was in it," one old man told me. "Not the story really at all, but the idea you were passing your time with the others. 'Twas like mass, you see, because we went to the chapel for the same reason."

I lament the passing of any art that was also a way of life.

"But there is a more deadly system at work now," returned the doctor. "The country is silently bleeding to death."

"Not to death," rejoined Hugh Kearney. "Those of her people who are forced to fly are not lost to Ireland. And those who cling to her are advancing in knowledge and intelligence. The people are becoming an educated and a thinking people. When Billy Heffernan's sons grow to manhood, they will in many respects be different men from their father."

— Charles J. Kickham, *Knocknagow*

There is now an arch of hardened clouds stretching across the entire sky. Tadhg says that this sort of formation is native to Connemara alone. How does he know? "An old traveling man told me, and he had been around all of Ireland."

Our talk is interrupted by the arrival of his son in a blue van with the message **KUNG FU YOU** painted on its backside in interlocking orange and yellow flowers, like the tangled beasts in the *Book of Kells*. As he pulls up, Tadhg mentions that Liam has just come from a visit with his mother in the Galway hospital. The bladder sickness, he says softly. A slight reddening in his face accompanies this statement. Has the connection of the bladder with its bodily function colored him like this? Or maybe whatever intercepts the orderly progress of family life is a source of some distress.

Liam greets me cheerfully. Right away, he wants to make a good impression. A rapport between us in these alien surroundings. He tells me of an accident he has just seen on the road outside Galway. Someone's motorcar smashed into a tinker's cart, disabling the horse. They had to shoot him, the horse. Incomprehensible people, those tinkers. Liam scoffs at their being allowed on the road at all "in this day and age."

I begin to see why his father defers to him. Not just because "Liam has the English, not myself, and he knows all the crafty ways of talking in it." It is manner: he may be "all shoes," but he is also a gush of nervous energy surging upward from the shoes. The runes of the city, where compacted things must aim at the sky, seem written on his mind. Much younger, he had applied his muscles to bull earth; now, at thirty, he seems to carry that same strength more formally within him, in his handshake, in his eyes. The density of his aggressiveness seems to pull everything toward him. People, I should think, must be pulled toward him too, for he is quite likable — and he knows it.

"Who'll be your next President, do you think?" he asks me with a somewhat prodding voice that implies he is not so much interested in an answer as he is in placing me alongside some aspiring Worthy, the better to gauge the content of my own aspirations.

We've given up on the President idea, I tell him.

And myself, I have few aspirations at the moment. Such as they are, they are contained in the attempt to unearth the sane social ethic once known in these desolate parts. And in animate contact with the last survivors of that ethic in the lifeboats of their crannied cabins. I stutter in trying to divulge this to Liam, and he clearly does not understand, and at last, failing all else, I invoke the mountains, the Twelve Bens of Connemara; they must have made the hard life here a bit easier, I say, but actually fail to say. But the reference to these mountains puts him in mind of the view from his guesthouse, and he begins to discuss his plans for the summer.

"The mountains, they're a grand thing to draw people in. And do you see the fresh air we have here? Each summer hundreds of visitors drive through this part of Galway and it's only a very limited accommodation we can give them. The visitor is the only hope in it, as near as I can see, because just about everything else here is dead. But there is opportunities, opportunities for a new beginning."

In a way, he is right. If the land can't produce, it must be sold — one way or the other. Yet after that, what of the people who perversely remain with it? Armed with only their spades, they'll be pommeled to death by battalions of outsiders — "the tourist class," as Liam calls them. That there can be tourists at all, given the necessity of those spades, seems a demoralizing thing.

Liam figures that he and his wife will make more than eight hundred pounds during the three summer months with this bed and breakfast operation. Not much, he says, but more than his father made any single year of his life selling milk to the creamery and kneading the soil to the consistency of ash. During the rest of the year, he will still have his Dublin job. His wife, a secretary with Aer Lingus, will be making money as well. "She's a student of art at the night program at University College," he says, and points to some of her handiwork, the flowered inscription on his van. I ask him about the origins of this motto he brings to the motorways of Ireland. "Oh, we love to watch all the Kung Fu films in Dublin. And James Bond, of course. Grand!"

"What's a James Bond?" Tadhg, silent and respectful until now, suddenly inquires. Alas, the dreadful backwardness has finally risen up in him to public exposure. Liam casts me a complicit smile, as though we both understood the old man to be slightly absurd. I return the smile, but it is aimed straight at the overfleshed shape of his vanity, which puts him above his father on so small an account. However, I can now see what Liam's aggressiveness has done: he has become the father, the man of the world. And Tadhg? He is the storyteller in the relationship, fastened forever to his own archaism. History dictates that he remain passive, like the land.

Inside the van is an entire outfitting of bathroom fixtures from Dublin ("You get the best deals on toilets in Dublin, you know") which Liam plans to install in the guesthouse this weekend. Bord Failte, the Irish Tourist Board, sanctions only guesthouses that have proper plumbing facilities. Grants from the board are even available to sanitary places like the one Liam will soon have. He hopes to get one of these grants, "the shit dole," he calls it. "They pay you so that your guests can move their bowels in comfort."

Liam smiles cheerily again as I start the work of unloading. "Careful, careful," he says. "You are holding the first toilet ever seen on our land." At this crack, Tadhg clicks his tongue with displeasure: Liam should know better than to air *that* piece of dirty laundry under my nose. But he grabs the other toilet, Tadhg does, and as we walk together toward the house, I glance at him and think, A shanachie bearing a toilet is an image of some truth.

The Tinker

Thaw! The last word in stolentelling!
— James Joyce, *Finnegans Wake*

We Could Have All Been Bards

These people prey on the tourists, and visitors think there's
only a bunch of tinkers down here. It's giving Galway a bad
name.
— former Mayor of Galway (quoted in the *Irish Times*)

AN UNTENANTED LOT beside a foundry in Sligo town: rusted
scraps of iron, giant fernery, a few wadded pages from the *Sligo
Champion,* empty bottles of stout and "100 Pipers" Scotch
Whiskey, an empty box of Jeyes Mansize Tissues, the defunct
body of an Austin Minor, scattered orange peels, several tins
depleted of their Batchelor's Peas long ago, a sweep's brush
battered beyond repair, broken glass, and a discarded billboard
advertising Player's Cigarettes, which are said to please; the

whey-headed girl-child of eleven or twelve, a bottle of Guinness resting between her hands, is seated on an old motor-car muffler listening to the ramblings of her elders. Eight or ten men and women have improvised a campfire amid this refuse. The scene is enough to draw a prolonged keen from the dedicated social worker; and a prolonged exegesis from the sociologist.

"Sure, we still have the 'reelies' now," one woman, bound by a nest of faded shawls, remarks of this fugitive gathering. At her feet is a muddy infant, gently asleep. She takes a draught from her bottle of Guinness, and her eyes close with a shudder of ecstacy.

I ask this woman where she got the Scottish word "reelies," and she replies, "Oh, I been travelin' the most of me life. Yer picks up things when yer travelin'."

"At night, when the poor farmer is sleepin', that's when she picks them up," a man roars, and there is a burst of laughter gathering the whole crowd of them together.

I have sat down with these "tinkers" because I happened to be passing on the street when a few words cradled in an antique brogue jumped out from this lot and astonished me:

"Yer a great storyteller, Winnie, bugger the rest."

"Bugger the King of Englnd, now."

"She's a Queen now, in Englnd."

"Well, bugger her, an' all her lords, dukes, an' earls."

"Bugger the whole fuckin' world."

"Aye."

When Liam Sugrue spoke with glee of the tinker and his shattered cart, he was only defending the point of view of his newly-acquired bathroom: that tinkers are filthy, primitive artifacts. For him, so are chamberpots. Other people, though, are more overt in the toiletry of their pronouncements. "Sewage, filthy scum, filthy riffraff," exclaimed a man in a western tourist office when I inquired where in his town I could find some of these traveling folk. He was not, I gathered, referring to the tourists. Later, when I asked a local tinker about this man's hostility, he shrugged and shook his head and said, not without a touch of irony, "Why, in me grandfather's time, that fellow's people sold their women to the British soldiers in the army garrison here."

Yet to some extent, they are dirty, in the way that people without adequate domestic facilities often are; and to the extent that a Bord Failte employee is civilized, tinkers are indeed primitive. But it is each generation's presumption to think of itself as less primitive than the one that preceded it, to consider itself more advanced because it is possessed of bigger cities and thicker jungles of man-eating technology. "I woulda gone t'work in London, an' I coulda gone," an old Galway tinker told me, "but I heard that it was a wild an' primitive place there." In certain barren locales, the old orders and rituals of cohesiveness have been swallowed up by mass culture; at least, that's what I take it this tinker meant, himself a part of a fiercely communal group, when he called London "a primitive place." Very big creatures have a way of not keeping the various sections of their bodies straight. There was never anything especially intelligent about the brontosaurus; it just had an insatiable appetite and a plodding yet inexorable manner: a late twentieth century beast.

In 1974, a member of Ballina's Urban Council suggested that all the traveling people be sterilized and then sent to the Aran Islands to live out their lives. This good councillor must have forgotten that, far from being a barbarous place entitled to the tinkers, the Arans have become a centerpiece for tourism in the West, attracting a thousand day-trippers from Galway of a summer's day. A sterilized tinker does not begin to evoke the same appeal for these tourists as a cart ride with an Aran jarvey around the island, past smiling children who charge just a few shillings to be photographed in their natural setting.

Hatred of the tinker, I think, is hatred of the past. The more violent it is, the greater the need to blot out past images, to lie about origins, to sever the connections between history and one's own person. To be anonymous. For tinkers are like survivals from past generations of rural Ireland, tattered and sustained by drinking, deposited on the self-regarding present by the warp of time and their traveling. Constant movement suspended their growth, and isolated them from the centers of money and knowledge; the endless road taught them perseverance. Owning very little, they clung to their natural customs as other people do to their possessions. And after a time, they came to be considered the people of another country (for the past is another country). An unearthly region where there are hexes and fortune telling, and a few men making things out of tin. A mysterious region: tinkers are somehow supposed to remain healthy by eating soot.

People walk up to them on the streets now, and ask to have their fortunes told, and the tinkers are only too glad to comply, for a few pence. "Yes, yer baby will be a boy." Yet such predictions are set pieces, offered impassively and from a distance — for the tinker looks upon the settled Irishman as a foreigner, too.

I have come to these traveling people (and not to the agents in the tourist offices stationed up and down the West like British garrisons in Zululand) to listen. Their stories are said to be good, which wouldn't be surprising, considering that their circumstances often compel them to take refuge in words. And in theft, which these days is nearly the same thing.

The name "tinker" did not give offense until quite recently. It derives from the sounds the tinsmith made at work, and a hammer striking metal was not an indecent sound for the longest time. But when the trade of tinsmithing floundered after the last war, the term started to be used against the remaining practitioners of it, to suggest that perhaps they had outlived their usefulness on earth. And now, with the trade nearly dead, "tinker" can be an insult, a sort of equivalent to "nigger," especially when it falls from the lips of a shopkeeper or publican. There is a young traveling man in Dublin who regularly takes the offending party to the courts if the word "tinker" ever so much as crosses his hearing. The 1963 *Report of the Commission on Itinerancy*, official concern written all through its pages, invented the more neutral words "itinerant" and "traveler" to attach to these people, and since then, those two words have become public domain, rallying cries that knit liberal brows. Yet when an older traveling man calls one of his comrades a "tinker," that is very nearly a term of endearment. For then it has a life-giving effect, as though thirty years of moribundity had been shattered with the tinkling of a word. I am using the word with this final shade of its meaning.

The generation sitting at this fire, mostly people in their forties and fifties, prefer "tinker" because of its familiarity. They do not exactly *like* the word, but it is what they've always been called. So it will suffice. Concerning the two recent substitutes for it, one man chortles, "Some shit will never flush." Though he is more pleased with that image than anything else, "itinerant" does exude a counterfeit elegance to him. "We used t'be called 'tinkers.' 'Course some of them is gettin' a bit genteel now and they likes the bigger words, like 'itin'runt.'" And I think "traveler" must conjure up an image for him of an English tourist sniffing the countryside for a bed and breakfast. Plainer words suit him better; unpaved roads, too, were once more appropriate to his movements.

Right now, released into drink, these people are hardly interested in pondering the question of nomenclature. They are sitting in this place of discards, discards themselves, and the exuberance of their talk tells me that they are happy. Slowly, I catch the story — first one man telling it, then another elaborating on what he's just said — of how this disheveled version of the outdoors got to be their drinking establishment.

For some time, the appearance of one or more of them in the bar of Kelleher's Hotel had put the fear of God in the management there. The wind was starting to flow between them and the bar's other patrons. "Us folks" were the barbarians at the gates, calling for their porter. Civilized people were starting to stay away; even, the uncivilized ones were looking askance at this flotsam of the road. Finally, these "lawless vagabonds" (as the newspapers often call them, apparently confusing them with Robin Hood's men) were refused service at the bar; yet, no harm, they could still buy drink to take away, which is what they do several times a week, consuming it here, "a great place." They do not tend to think of this treatment as objectionable, except in the rain.

" 'Tis baycause we're a right drunken curse of God crowd. Odd t'say, them what goes inta the hotel bars today goes there t'get sober, not drunk like ourselves," says Winnie O'Brien. She would often make off with the sample cases of commercial travelers who'd stop in Kelleher's for a bit of sustenance between sales.

Then, Anne O'Brien, Winnie's daughter, would often go inside to beg with her baby swathed in rags, cajoling likely strangers with "Misther, could y' gimme somethin' for the wee wan t'asn't et in t'ree days?" When refused her half crown, she'd deposit the baby in the victim's lap, saying, "Here, y'take care of him, then."

With pints on him, Michael McCarthy would use the opportunity to punch one of his comrades. He insists that he has never "laid me fisht" to anyone other than another traveling person.

Biddie Ward would try to sell used clothing "t'the gentry that would gather inside."

"Big John" Lawrence, a barge of a man, once threatened one of the Wards with what the local newspaper identified as "a touch of Kung-fu — two batonlike sticks joined by a short chain," but threw this instrument of torture to the floor as the two of them "struck each other with their fists and got into grips with one another."

Anthony Lawrence once crashed an empty bottle of Guinness against the juke box when the publican told him he already had "too much drink taken." "I only let me own people tell me that."

Anthony's wife Teresa would mix drink and strange language in a fashion unacceptable to delicate ears.

Packy Ward would never participate in any of these rows, but he was not beneath removing odd items of furniture from the premises while one was in progress. But for this technique, his house would be mostly bare.

Patsy Flynn, the loser in this arrangement, was guilty by association. "The boozin'" had never affected him one way or the other. If it did not drive him, as it did the others, to acts of an antisocial nature, neither did it impel him to that overripe sociability that often hastens a brawl. "I stop at eight pints, that's me limit."

It is in such acts of cunning and violence that these people, the oddments of perhaps the very old aristocracy of Ireland, respond to the present moment. And in telling jokes at the expense both of themselves and "the buffers" (the settled population), they turn away the time that crowds them into the vacant lots beyond respectability. Into those scraps of abandonment that fairly describe the public attitude toward them. Nowadays, they are at one with nature only in places where nature has been written off as a loss.

This campfire itself helps point to something essential for them. Though the afternoon air presses the skin with a warmth that makes fires redundant, it is the ritual of assemblage, not the heat, that matters. The fire, with the force of a magnet over steel filings, draws them here as to some remote, pleasing memory. It creates a community dissolving all loss of community beyond the space of its heat.

But a campfire represents a relapse, of a sort. In the contemporary past, ten years ago and more, it would have rewarded a day's efforts with a "budget" pack wherein a man attempted to barter a few antiquated skills for a little money, or better, a cabbage and some spuds. Today, in the middle of a town the size of Sligo, it is a positive eccentricity. Because the O'Briens, the Wards, the Lawrences, and the McCarthys are no longer "on the road," except for occasional scrap-dealing forays, and "the road," in any event, is no longer "open" like it once was, with wide margins where a tent could be pitched and horses could wander. On a narrow road, the motorcar will assassinate a tinker's cart. So the County Council has put them into cramped *tigins*, pseudohouses that are a step toward legitimate settlement; if they respond decently to these dwellings, if they do not attempt to make them conform more to nature through small acts of house destruction, then they become eligible for tenement flats, which are a step toward oblivion. The Lawrences inhabit a flat near Kelleher's Hotel. The rest of them are still at the *tigín* stage, and their houses have been dispersed to the four corners of Sligo in an effort to dismantle the clannishness that this fire, temporarily, is restoring to them.

Drink, too, gives them a united front, and it also drives them apart, but when it does that, it solidifies them in their respective clans, and then, woe to the McCarthy from whom a Ward has purchased an imperfect horse on good faith. Duplicity like that usually results in a man defending the blood of his clan with his own flesh, fighting from one stupor until he's bashed into another. Brawling is a very old virtue from pre-industrial times; it brings into hand-to-hand contact people who would otherwise have been ciphers to each other. In the old hero tales, it has the desirability of love.

Only drink can make them heroic nowadays. Only the imbibing of what "Big John" Lawrence calls "God in a bottle" can sponge away the dusty burden of being alive at the wrong time, a burden so overwhelming perforce none of them is able to talk of it. Yet, as "Big John" says, it is very traditional with them to improve their minds with great amounts of drink: "Not long ago, when there wasn't houses for us in it at all, there was nothin' you could spend yer money on but drink. You wouldn't buy chairs or beds or this sort of thing, baycause you hadn't the house t'put them in. Drink would give you anythin' you wanted, in yer mind, like. Even wit' houses now, they still stick t'the old custom of spendin' all their money on drink. I think meself that a good pint is better than anything you could put in a house, don't you?" For him, drink is a rapid transit to the interior life; the interior furnishings of a house are, well, not connected with the interior life. The tedium of possessions: the tinkers get tired of their things quickly, and trade them away and then trade what they get for them away. "Big John" owns three wrist watches; he got them for a concertina, which he had gotten for a bicycle, for which he had traded a new set of chimney-sweeping brushes. "I figured the day of the sweep, it would soon be over."

Lacking property, these people lack the acquisitor's proper respect for it. To cast a stone through a shop's window is no different from casting it into a field after a rabbit; farmers don't claim the rabbits that undermine their fields as their own possessions.

And God created objects to turn them into fire. For example: A rotted fence encloses these grounds, and Teresa Lawrence has just kicked a gray slat from it, the one on which is imprinted **PRIVATE PROPERTY.** She whacks it against a large stone, throwing the slivered pieces into the campfire. She can't read, but since the written word to her mind exists only to tell her what she cannot do, where she can't drink or put up a "temporary dwelling," it doesn't matter.

The rest of the group have a good laugh at Teresa's decision to place this fence at the disposal of their fire. But they don't seem to realize the precise beauty of burning **PRIVATE**

PROPERTY. Sitting by himself, Patsy Flynn merely smiles. He *can* read. Still, some years ago he couldn't read either "good, bad, or indiff'runt," and he mentions that he once tethered his horse to a **NO PARKING** sign outside the town of Tuam. "I thought that the sign said you could tie yer horse there, see," he says. The syntax of his face barely moves: his education came too late to prevent him from being here.

Anthony Lawrence's two little girls are ripping fiercely at each other's frocks. In a fit of jealousy, the younger one has just kicked over the older girl's bottle of cider because their father had spiked it with whiskey, ignoring her own, and now she is defending herself against a physical assault. "You little tinker bitch," she screams at her sister after her right side has been laid bare to the waist. A soft breeze shivers the sea bottom of ferns, and Anthony, ignoring his fighting daughters, begins to talk with disgust of a certain local shopkeeper who has a mastiff on the premises to keep the tinkers away. This dog recently bit one of his daughters when she entered the shop for a stick of candy.

Suddenly, Winnie O'Brien wonders what has become of Packy Ward. He is supposed to be delivering additional Guinness from Kelleher's, and he has been gone far too long. "He'd be a good messenger t'send for death," she comments. Several pairs of eyes look with approval on her: she has just hatched a bon mot.

In her late fifties, Winnie looks at least twenty years older. On her face is compressed the cumulative weight of having to bear "sixteen childher, an' only eight of them still in it." The honey of peace is not to be found in her eyes. Her features are so wind-whipped and striated, Jacob Epstein would have needed to add nothing to them: in these features, one sees the contours of a rural geography, roads and winding rivers and hillocky rises, and not really the ravages of time. Such skin as she does possess, stretched to its papery limits, is more than a man can envy.

Winnie remains the constant delight of this group. They are entertained by her resourcefulness and general waggishness.

They defer to her when she starts to speak, and they watch her when she starts to move. Her body may look frail, but there is still a defiant crispness in her use of it.

A "dudeen," a small clay pipe, is tucked behind her ear, beneath the hair. She tells me that she hates smoking it, but she'll do it anyway if she thinks someone in the streets will be charmed enough for this hearkening back to the "Ould Oireland." In begging, she is just as calculating. She reels off stories so patently absurd that she is often rewarded for her performance more than her sorrowful bearing: "Will y'gimme a half crown, misther, for t'send me four stupid sons t'be eddicated at Trinity College?" These appeals, which she knows no one believes, give her the opportunity to match wits with the settled population. She aims straight for their ideal of upward mobility. Her own sense of mobility takes a different direction, leading on a level from one place to the next, going nowhere.

"Tell us a story, tell us a story, Winnie," chant two of the children, who have been throwing empty bottles into the fire.

She accommodates them immediately, launching into a boozy monologue the principal topic of which is indeed the recent peregrinations of her own boozy cunning. Ending with:

". . . a man is a man, anyway, an' this last fellow gave me a drink for nothin'. 'Twas just this Friday last. He was a big man wit' a big saloon car, a lovely car. 'Hello,' he said t'me. 'How y'doin', misther,' says I. ' 'Tis a great day.' ' 'Tis a great day,' says I. 'Yer a great talker,' he says. 'Not so bad at all, but come here,' says I t'im, an' I says, 'Do you know what you can do for me?' An' he dasn't, bless him, he dasn't know! So I says, 'For the love of God, sir, will y'gimme ten bob for a coupla bottles of stout, an' I'll say a prayer for yer!' 'If yer as good a singer as a talker, I'll give it t'yer.' 'I'm a singer the likes of which y'ave never sane before,' says I. So we wint t'Michael Henry's, no, James Henry's pub, an' I says t'im, I says, 'I'll stand outside the door, 'cause if yer ashamed wit' me t'gwin, I'll stand outside.' 'Not at all,' he says. 'Gwin.' So he left down half dozen of stout an' I said, 'That's very nice an' thanks an' God bless.' 'Oh for God's sakes, sing,' says he. 'Well, gimme a whiskey an' I'll sing anythin' you want,' says I. 'A whiskey, then,' he says. 'Gwon, drink up that then an' sing,' says he. 'Gwon.' 'Well, I never sang in me whole life,' I says t'im, an' up an' walked out."

"With the stout," reminds one of the children. The gist of the story is in the public domain.

"Wit' the stout," Winnie says in triumph.

"Y'd want t'be middlin' cute for that make of man," says her daughter Anne.

"Y'd want fine wits in yer head, all right," she says. Drink has saturated her Muse irreparably, but she still has conferred on this mere "crack" some of the measured sanctity of the wonder tale. She cannot help it; she is a Grand Dame infused with Guinness, and experience comes to her begging to be parlayed into an anecdote.

This is the last recourse of storytelling in Winnie's generation: to skewer the "buffers." Their plots all focus on that. The story possibilities are limited, but they at least clarify this late urban world, locating identities that would otherwise be lost to slum housing. In the retelling of such incidents, they disavow the covering of city cement, the most stifling of all underbrush. Let it be banal, the theft of a roll of toilet tissue, and all the better, it will be turned into a pitched battle between themselves and the "buffers." The results will be a story which makes them seem like Finn McCool's men toying with a militia of mongoloids. Real life is just as merciless; there, however, they themselves are the victims and they drizzle from street to street in the winter of their ruin, ignoring words because they cannot read them.

At last Packy Ward returns with the extra supply of stout.

"Do y'like t'let the grass grow under yer feet, then?" someone asks him.

Packy scowls, and his hair, which naturally sticks out like a thistle, seems to stick out all the more. As it turns out, he has been followed by one of the guards, Guard Kearney, they all know him, a terrible man for harassment. To divert him from their unauthorized assembly, he, Packy, has had to trek over half of Sligo with the stout in his hands.

None of them is sure that he hasn't instead supped a few inaugural drinks with some of the McDonoughs just arrived from Galway and pulled up in their caravan on the Ballina road. But they quickly take the bottles he offers them.

Anthony Lawrence and Michael McCarthy begin to reflect upon the recent death in Loughrea of "King" Ward, "the king of the tinkers" and the pride of the Ward clan, a man of vast generosity who would never have kept his comrades waiting for a drink. These two men were at the king's funeral, along "wit' ev'ry son of a tinker in this country," the news of his death having spread faithfully from family to family (none of whom own telephones). They puzzle themselves with the thought of names, other than those of the old and infirm, which were conspicuous by their absence. Finally, Michael mentions a Ballina man he hadn't seen there, but "he's becomin' a reg'lar nuisance, wit' money in the bank an' all."

There is accord between them: the media publicity given the king contributed in some obscure fashion to his downfall. Michael says that the tinkers no more require a king than do the Irish people at large. This idea of a king was the invention of "the eejots wit' the newspapers" who thought it would be "cute" if the tinkers had a king. As if they really didn't obey any laws but their own. Then, Michael says, having built him up, the newspaper proceeded to tear him down again. "They showed a picture of him in front of his little house in Loughrea. He was comin' out in the morning after bein' drunk the most of the night, it looked like. They said 'This is the King of the Tinkers in his castle.' Flashed him with the camera all boozed up, poor fellow."

I read his meaning: the king died of exposure.

"But he was a fine lad of a man, anyway!" Anthony exclaims.

"An' he idled what time he was given, rest him," Michael says. "They say that when a man of his sort dies, he will turn inta an old mule an' carry the Orangeman inta Hell."

Then the two of them fall into a heated debate on the virtues and flaws of going up to Belfast, in order to purchase furnishings from bomb-damaged pubs and sell them as antiques in the Republic. Their feelings are not much affected by the "troubles" in the North; they have their own troubles.

Pleaze Do Not Run Over Childrun or Horses
— sign by a roadside encampment of Galway
tinkers awaiting settlement

These traveling people, their travels at an end, inhabit two worlds, the one buried and the other perpetually unborn. The twisted geometries of scrap objects must suffice for their countryside; and their campfires are clandestine now. At their age, with their skills, they are hardly assimilable; they lack the education to be insurance agents and they haven't enough savoir faire to serve Bord Failte in any capacity. The only hope is for their children, who still have the chance to grow up and be like everyone else.

Like the Irish-speaking pockets of the West, the traveling people are a small nation cloaked by a larger one. This nation includes approximately fourteen hundred families, with an indeterminate number of children, who are not always registered, the assumption being that if simple baptism was good enough for their parents, it should be good enough for them. These families are larger now than they ever were before, as though they're arming themselves through youthful reinforcement against a possible purge. Still, the increase of his tribe has always been a matter of considerable importance to the traveling person. Perpetuating his own name, a man attains himself in all his power and glory. The craving for progeny — it has very little to do with sexual self-esteem — reflects an almost holy attitude toward clan and heredity. It goes back to the time when the country was just a collection of warring clans and a chieftain's family and his soldiery were one and the same. Even today, onto the lives of the few tinkers who remain unmarried is inscribed a stigma something like excommunication.

The clan is money in stressful times, when an errant stone has shattered a confectioner's window, and it is mutual aid, when a mountain of scrap needs collecting, and it is a song in the backbone, chanting of body parts that connect so neatly. Clans *feud,* they don't compete; and feuding clansmen have a closer relation to each other than they do to people on the outside with whom they are on remote good terms. In this world, the urge toward competition has never dictated behavior, family groups will tarmac a road together or they will battle each other over a humiliated girl or a stolen horse, but they will never, never go into business against each other. Private enterprise is not their bag of oats. They are more accustomed, even in the staging of a brawl, to the spirit of cooperation. This is why many of them suffer unusual withdrawal symptoms trying to adjust to urban "society," which is competitive, not social in the way that their own lives have always been; window breaking has, in fact, become very popular with them as of late.

On the pre-industrial lifeways of the West, these people themselves are like a window. Despite its apparent fragility, their window has managed to stay intact, if somewhat smudged, and through it, there is the blurred prospect of the old self-contained life of the country, the communal ethic, the tolerance of eccentricity, vital words. I think of Seán Murphy, and Tadhg Sugrue and then I think of these traveling people. They are really tribal units of the same world, though almost all of them have left it now for the cities and towns, where they've come for some of the same reasons as other country people — the faster pace, employment, and a higher dole allotment when there is no employment. But their work habits, on those occasions when work they can perform is offered them, remain pre-industrial with a vengeance; they prefer piecework to wages and they would no more think of laboring for a deferred reward than of operating guesthouses. About the closest they ever come to capitalism is in the shabby stalls they sometimes set up on the outskirts of a town in order to hawk umbrellas, religious icons, and used clothing. But this is just a more sophisticated version of "tinkering."

Not having Irish, the tinkers cannot get the language grants received by denizens of the Gaeltacht. However, the older ones among them still have *Shelta*, or "cant" in the vernacular, a concoction of seventeenth century sham Latin, Romani (the gypsy tongue), English, and old Irish. "Big John" Lawrence: "There was a tinkerman who said t'Cromwell, 'Your gris to the mídil.' When Cromwell asked him t'translate it, your man wouldn't, so he said, 'I can't,' and that's why it's called 'cant' today. What did he mane by those words? 'Your soul to the Devil.'" This "cant" is like a back slang. The tinkers use it mostly in the presence of a "straight" person, to communicate troublesome information to each other. Like "The glócates are suni'n for you." (The police are looking for you). For obvious reasons, the Irish government chooses not to reward this sort of thing with stipends.

The daily language of the tinkers is the countryman's English of perhaps a hundred years ago. Up until now, their journeyings had insulated them against the standardized English taught in the national schools; they could hardly know that talk is supposed to be pale and wan. Literacy, which can paralyze speech with propriety, was never needed in their lives. On the road, it would not refine the making of tinware, nor would it pitch a wattle tent or help put the canvas over that tent's hooped branches. But now, for the first time in the history of their world, to read and write is to enter life; the older ones have chosen settlement on account of their children, who they rightly perceive would be at a greater disadvantage without education than they themselves could ever be. At the end of the road, there is no place to go but the schoolhouse.

A few of them even regret not being able to read or write themselves.

"If I was eddicated," says Winnie O'Brien, "I'd write meself a big book on the origins of the travelin' people. I heard a good many stories about that from me mother, who got them from her mother, that it'd be an awful shame that they'd be lost for the rest of time."

Yet Winnie is preliterate, not illiterate: her mind's frame of reference pays no heed to the recent invention of the printing press. She goes back to the time of talking.

Winnie's people have wandered the road longer than their own memories permit them to imagine, and each step has borne them further from whoever it was that invented them. Probably, there was no single inventor; no single accurate explanation of their origins. One theory makes them the native Irish aristocrats from the period of the Cromwellian plantations; dispossessed, they continued to skulk the peripheries of their ancestral holdings, deteriorating with the years. "Big John" says that his own family doesn't go farther back in time than the Famine, at which time they were evicted by cruel landlords in County Mayo. And another theory identifies the traveling people as the descendants of those medieval bards who never stopped walking even after their roaming bardic services were no longer needed.

Packy Ward finds this last answer as good as any. His own family name derives from *Mac an Bhaird,* which in Irish means "Son of the Bard." He is grateful to me for giving him that piece of information. "We could have all been bards, so we could," he observes.

I want to hear Winnie telling another story.

I want to determine whether she has a few of the traditional tales in her repertoire, and while I'm puzzling myself over the best means of approaching her for this, given her present level of intoxication (which needn't dampen a story, particularly with a teller otherwise inhibited), a sudden hush settles over the proceedings. Guard Kearney has arrived. In his face is a politeness born of resignation. Hands on his hips, he assumes the attitude of a kindly schoolmaster who knows his pupils are hopeless.

You will all have to move on, Guard Kearney says. He points to the hole in the fence, which serves as a gate, as though none of this crowd would know the precise method of getting out.

Move on, now.

You, John, move on.

On with you now, Winnie.

No trouble, please.

Move on, Michael.

Move on.

Then he sees me, and is a little perplexed. *I* am no tinker. But he soon smiles. He tells me I'd be allowed to stay here . . . if I want.

The Road Is the Best College

> For peregrination charms our senses with such unspeakable
> and sweet variety, that some count him unhappy that never
> travelled, a kind of prisoner, and pity his case that from his
> cradle to his old age beholds the same still; still, still the same,
> the same.
> — Robert Burton, from *The Anatomy of Melancholy*

A TOURIST COACH slashes by, filled with mannequin faces and heading for Yeats' grave in Drumcliff.

Shortly after I step out onto the street, Packy Ward intercepts me. He has been waiting for my reentry into downtown Sligo. He reaches with birdlike delicacy into his pouch of a coat pocket, and removes a small radio. He assures me that it isn't a hot item. In fact, he got it from a farmer for a donkey in the early stages of decrepitude. Not a bad exchange for either party, he says, because the donkey could still perform a few good days of work before turning in its harness, and the radio — he holds it up for my close scrutiny — well, it hasn't died yet.

Now the point is, would I like to trade my tape recorder for this little radio? Packy flicks it on, and from a thicket of static emerges a Dublin accent battling to imitate an American country-western vocal style . . .

"Down at dis troock shtop in my own home town
I met my gal in me bes' friend's arrims . . ."

He nods. Good stuff, eh?

I have to tell him that I won't barter my tape recorder. Not even for a comparatively energetic donkey much less his radio. But he isn't disappointed at this; what he really wants is just to hear "that little yoke" (thing). Machines entrance him.

I switch on the recorder. From Connemara, the voice of Tadhg Sugrue is saying: ". . . if it's storytellers you want, it's twenty years too late you've come . . . The day of the storyteller is over . . . 'Tis now the day of . . . I don't know . . . I don't know what it's the day of . . ."

Packy stares at the machine and then at me. Do I want *storytellers?* Well, he can take me directly to the best storyteller ever heard in these parts. ". . . it's me own father, Mickey Ward. He's a great man for stories. Why sure, he'd build a nest in yer ear. He lives next to me, in a caravan out Ben Bulben way."

I ask him what sort of stories.

Oh, just lies and other old stories, he says. Is there any difference? At any rate, he cannot mince words on such things. He offers me a weak-shouldered shrug, as if to say, Vanity, vanity, all is vanity. And with that, he has dropped the slight interest he had in the subject of stories. For now, could he hold my tape recorder, just to see how it works?

"You should get me father. I'd like t'hear his voice speakin' on this yoke. Oh, I'd like it well."

Together we walk toward Ben Bulben, stopping only for a

priest who wonders if Packy's little boy has recovered from his recent illness. "I believe he'll get better soon, Father. 'Tis just a touch of pneumonia, that's all."

We turn down one boreen and then another, and there our destination is, tucked safely away from public view, a little isolated community of three jerry-built *tigíns*. Off by itself is a caravan. To call it a "mobile home," however, would be a misnomer. The wheels have been removed, rendering it helpless. Its dents and discolorations give it the look of a bad skin disease. It is like a contemptible leviathan rejected by the sea, washed up on a strand from which the tide has now receded. Packy points to it; there, in that tinny compartment, lives his father.

Inside the caravan, an elderly man with a notched twig in his hand is engaged in putting a straw crucifixion scene, piece by piece, into an empty whiskey bottle. Speaking with characteristic jauntiness, Packy introduces me to "Mickey Wilberforce Ward, the last of the storytellers." Then he departs.

"I amn't the last of anything" is Mickey's first observation, once we are alone. The bottom of his face is collapsed and rubbery. It will be the last face he ever owns; it could well be the last face ever composed completely by the life of the road, its development unchecked by walls. I am held to his face by his eyes, his dancing eyes, which are blue as periwinkles.

He will leave the world poorer by these eyes, at least.

Sligo is Yeats country, so travel brochures warn the unsuspecting, and to educated people, such an affiliation has a certain truth to it. Sligo's landscape can be seen in terms of Yeats. Drumcliff, the Lake Isle of Innisfree (which locals call Rat Island), Dooney Rock, and the right-angled precipice of Ben

Bulben — they are not without a certain significance to those who, as the tinkers say, "trade in them yokes."

Mickey Ward, when I ask him if he's heard of Yeats, replies: "I knowed a man named Bobby Yeats once, was a gelder of pigs. But that was long ago."

"A *poet?* I knowed several poets in me time — Patrick Simpson, Jack Butler — all among the travelin' class. Jim Holden, sure, he was a born poet. He used t'make up songs of hurlin' teams an' murder cases years an' years ago."

Elsewhere in Sligo, the name of Yeats may be tossed around like a piece of snuff at a wake, but Mickey, like Winnie O'Brien, belongs to a much earlier day, long before the time the lank, mystical poet stepped to Sandymount to be born. In 1923, when Yeats was in Stockholm to receive the Nobel Prize, Mickey was trekking the West with his father, a tinsmith and chimney sweep, and inclining his ears to what he calls "the lovely old yarns." "I took more yarns inta me head than prayers. I took in so many, y'couldn't take them all away wit' an ass an' cart." Nor has Mickey ever received a prize for these "yarns" — for which he is thankful, knowing that if he did, he'd be held up for ridicule among his own people. They'd call him "proud" even if the prize wasn't his own fault. They'd think he was extending himself beyond his, their, limits. The glances of a well-scrubbed citizenry tell them that, as tinkers, they are all but unredeemable.

But like Yeats, Mickey is currently camped under Ben Bulben, or near it. His encampment is also more or less permanent, and he hates it. He'd rather be out on the road; he'd rather have a direct contact with the elements, "the terrible wet an' all." He shakes the sleeve of my coat to emphasize this fact.

"I traveled ev'ry art an' part of Galway an' Mayo, an' most of Sligo an' Leitrim. I was reared t'the road, an' outside is where I spent the time God gave me. But here, I'm not content here. Every day is a week t'me when I'm in this caravan. It's the same as gaol t'me; I'd imagine I'd be as well in gaol as wit' a few years here. Or as well down below in the county home, wit' all the old people, sick an' dyin'. The road is the best college. The best when yer brought up t'it. You'd see strange things. God, would you see strange things! You'd see something here now today, an' a diff'runt thing tomorrow, in a diff'runt place, an' you'd hear diff'runt little things, but you'll hear nothing in the wan place, when you'd be seein' all the wan thing. Jesus, Mary, an' Joseph, I find it very comical an' awk'rd t'be confined in the wan place."

Much of this is unreconstructed traveling man. Undoubtedly, much of it is also wistful memory-man. But I can see where this caravan would turn a person's mind to moods of grimness. Its small size allows very little room for movement; but it is still large enough, on this bright March afternoon, to keep the light from penetrating more than a few feet into its interior. Here, Mickey's want of assets is conspicuous in a way it never would have been on the road, when his assets consisted of everything around him. "When yer all the time movin', it's all the outside that you own." Part of his complaint, too, may come from loneliness; his wife died soon after they moved into this box of a home.

Mickey's tenure here has been slightly less than four years. Packy and his six children are stuffed into one of the *tigíns;* there are McCarthys and Lawlesses in the other two. Originally, Mickey himself was scheduled for a *tigín,* but he protested so roundly against life in one of "them gaols," suggesting a simple shakedown of straw instead, that he was awarded this caravan with the hope that its illusion of movement would quiet him down. "I told them that I wouldn't give wan tent, an' I'd sleep on a bed of straw, for the king's palace," he says. An image forms in my mind of him standing before the staid gray men of the County Council, lecturing them on the uninhabitability of human dwellings.

His seven pounds a week Labor Exchange money must help reconcile him to being grounded, hedgeless and forlorn, under Ben Bulben's head. Without a fixed abode, he wouldn't get a penny of it. He is at pains to explain, however, that this is not the old-age pension. He would never want *that*. It's only unemployment money; after all, he could still work if there was work to be got. So, he protests, it's not really his fault.

I think that this exile from work, because of his age and the fact that his skills are unfashionable, must affect him rather like the loss of his wife. He still repairs the occasional umbrella, dabbles in tinware, and these last few weeks he's been putting crucifixions into bottles, for Packy to hawk by the roadside. But these activities are just a substitute for work. Not that he isn't specialized enough to get work; on the contrary, he is *too* specialized in too many things. In the manner of his work, he suggests a small-scale Renaissance man, a Leonardo of the roads. His tinker's heritage locates him practically everywhere: in tinsmithing, cart building, blacksmithing, chimney sweeping, harness making, farm laboring, and of course in "horses, the king of the beasts." To observe him train a wild yearling is to see a work of art so perfectly choreographed, it would satisfy Aristotle's requirements for a beginning, a middle, and an end. But he never would have heard of Aristotle.

That is, Mickey's heritage locates him everywhere except where it matters right now. It was the subsistence occupation he mastered, the job that met the requirements of the immediate pre-industrial moment ("A tape recorder? How do them things work?"), and now, when motorcars smash the last wooden carts, subsistence is no longer possible. Horses, around which a whole way of life was built, are now only competitive playthings running in the Sweepstakes; they require a different sort of shoe from the workhorse, one with little durability, needing to last only a race or two. "Once," Mickey laments, "there was almost more horses in it than there was people."

Perhaps because his practiced hands have always exercised the divers demands put to them with such efficacy, Mickey refers to himself as "a queer old hwoor." "There now, amn't I a queer old hwoor?" he says, after remarking that he was once so talented with tin, "I could turn a needle into an anchor." Or that in his time he could "get up an' make a harness wit' any harness maker." He knows — he cannot help but know, unemployable as he is — that a person who can do these things is no longer of much use. In his world, the useless object, the broken horseshoe or even the broken-down horse, has always passed from view with the ease of a burial. What's "queer" about him is that he has survived long enough to witness his own impracticality — why wasn't he discarded long ago?

And in his own argot, to "whore" is human, possibly divine. On the road, the man of easy virtue could always feed his family better than the saint. He could, for example, "play the barrel" at a country fair. At such events, his wife would sell timber balls or sticks the size of chair legs to local people, and then the tinker would crouch inside a barrel, peering out a half-opening and ducking down again, while these nearly lethal items were thrown at him. Roars of approval from an assemblage of spectators would betoken a direct hit, human flesh exchanged for a few coppers. Mickey: "I sane it many times in the Galway races, they'd get him there on the forehead, knocked him unconscience." The woman's corresponding "job of work" was called "Moll of the Wad": "She'd sit in a ring, an' a pad propped on her backside, an' then they'd strike that wit' a great big mallet an' try t'drive her outa the ring, all the big strong men would try t'drive her outa the ring."

These sports of the fairs were common whorish occurrences, where the tinkers would quite literally act out the local hostility to them. And yet, this to them was life, whereas the assembly line was not. Mickey's own generation is too old to have served time in an Irish factory. Though they prostituted themselves to work in a variety of ways, they never saw the inside of an English factory. The manure of the roads would have been a violet by comparison.

Mickey is back talking about his Labor Exchange money. He mentions that a lot of hard workers are receiving it, and repeats several other facts about it, until he has given his acceptance of this dole money the effect of dignity. Packy says that this money appeals to him because it doesn't remind him of his age like the old-age pension would. Yet as far as his age is concerned, he will never be precisely reminded of it; having been self-employed his whole life, he has never been invited to come forth with a birth certificate. Maybe he is seventy, "but I could be sev'nty-t'ree, too." And anyway, he observes, tinkers are not supposed to live as long as everyone says he has lived. If asthma doesn't get them, arthritis will; if arthritis doesn't get them, the motorcar will. Mickey gets up from his bed, and to prove his great youth, he begins performing a succession of "shoot-the-cannons" on his caravan floor. "I got that trick off a returned Yank at the Ballinasloe Fair in about 1927."

Time must have touched his bones tenderly to let him do such physical exercising. But as I watch him bounce up and down, nimble as a boy, I sense that he's trying to prove something there is no need to prove: that he is still very much alive. This "trick," which requires all the parts of his body to work together, shows him straining to transcend caravan paralysis, if not to batten these four constricting walls down with the ram of his legs. I remember his unflattering comparison of this caravan with an Old Folks' home, and I find myself thinking, On this sunny day, he's trying to rid himself of the night thought that he's become gracelessly old. He is trying to make of his mind something other than a wheelless caravan.

I've noticed a good many country people like him, men and women who haven't necessarily lived longer than their counterparts elsewhere but who do seem to have preserved their vitalities for a longer time. It may be that they're able to hold themselves up to their own expectations longer because they aren't too often confronted with images lecturing them on how to be old. The Irish media hasn't yet emerged with the archetype of old people as charming, gay, incontinent children queuing up for the grave. And most sentient people view the County Home as the very worst thing that could befall them. Mickey has equated it with "gaol," yet in the County Home, it is really the mind that is the most unfortunate prisoner, surrounded as it is by images of permanent frailty. There couldn't

be a starker example of usefulness outlived. And of people losing the last ghost of their self-reliance. In this latter respect, a
County Home is rather like the Common Market. There, too, a
person is thrust into the hands of alien, antiseptic hands.

Again and again, I keep returning to old men. They have
triumphed to become dignified; maybe that's why I keep coming back. Diseases like self-absorption and ulcers sieve away the
weaker members of the species — old men are those who survive all kinds of famine. They have grown large enough to
contain lives besides their own. In Galway, I once saw a young
man in a business suit spitting on a somewhat disheveled tramp
who was trying to beg from him, and I remember thinking, An
old man would never do that. An old man would have understood more of what it means to go begging.

To some skin, there is also given a geography, which says, It
is implausible to live beyond the effects of the weather. The
lines on Mickey's own face, deeper than any imprint of words
on paper, have replaced the ability to write; they are a kind of
literacy in themselves, and a precise report of the weather. In
the end, such faces exist far away from the mundane process of
aging. There is simply too much landscape in them. Instead,
they seem to have taken it upon themselves to exhibit a whole
dying world in their features. For the old men of the West were
old at the beginning of their lives.

Mickey is executing the last of his "shoot-the-cannons." He is
breathing heavily, and as he pauses for a moment, his feet thrust
out behind him, there is a knocking at his caravan door. "Come
in, don't knock, only the police knocks," he shouts, and at that
point, a nun enters. She is Sister Margaret from Sligo, the local

liaison between the traveling people and the outside world, seeing to their health and general welfare; it is her wiles that get them to visit the doctor, whom they have always distrusted, preferring their own more traditional, cheaper remedies.

"Oh Sister," Mickey exclaims, scrambling to his feet, embarrassed to be caught in this compromising position on the floor. But she is all cheer and understanding; while she may not know exactly what he's doing there on the floor, she is pleased to see him occupied, occupied at *anything*. She even gestures him, in a brief tempest of confusion, back to the floor. She was only just checking in to say hello after dropping off a basket of clothing at his son's house. She is almost apologetic.

Mickey smiles at her. He is finished with his exercises, he says, and is almost apologetic himself. Most of the casualness has been choked from her visit by now, and with a genial swivel of her head, Sister Margaret turns to me; odd, I don't *look* like an "itinerant."

After I have told her the point of my own visit, she suggests that I see an "example" of traveling people successfully adjusting to the circumstances of settlement. She volunteers to introduce me to the adjustees themselves. This I take to be a quite unintentional slight of Mickey, who is as remote from this sort of adjustment as he is from a seat in the Dáil Eireann, the Irish Parliament. Thoughts of integration do not, to put it mildly, pull his horse cart.

Yet how can I refuse her eagerness, her desire to see these people content? I take leave of Mickey for the present, telling him that I'll be back later for a story, perhaps this evening, and he replies softly, so Sister Margaret won't hear him, "You won't get any stories where yer goin', that's for sure." We drive back through Sligo until we reach the southern suburbs, then negotiate an unpaved road, rutted with tire treads, past a blacksmith's ruined forge and what appears to be a town dump. Ben Bulben's massive scarp, which had disappeared, suddenly bulks again in the distance.

"Art Lawless is a petrol-pump attendant and a very good

mechanic at Slattery's garage in town. His wife is a chamber-maid at Dillon's hotel," Sister Margaret says as we pull up in front of a trim little bungalow with clipped hedges separating it from a farmer's pasture lands. On the front lawn, two plastic flamingos are drinking from a birdbath. Not more than twenty paces from the front step, in a neighboring field, a half dozen heifers are grazing with their calves.

This bungalow has been put out to pasture. It is behind everything; behind the town, behind its suburbs, behind even the local dump. It seems to dwell among farm animals, having established a peaceful coexistence with only these cows.

"We couldn't find a place where the neighbors wouldn't object to itinerants moving in on them," Sister Margaret says with an abrupt hardness to her voice.

Art Lawless emerges from beneath a Vauxhall Firenza ("The transmission's gone. Bad news.") to greet us. He is no more than twenty-two or twenty-three, and there is an open-aired freshness about him, a touch of brashness in his eyes. He is surprisingly clean for just having worked under a defective sports car. Hardly any oil stains spot his Mick Jagger T-shirt, which he got in England, he tells me, during a "fabulous" year he spent there "muckin' about."

"Art sometimes takes cars home from the garage to work on them in his spare time," Sister Margaret explains. With this insight into Art's diligence, is she trying to relieve me of whatever dark thoughts I might have on his method of acquiring this expensive car? I already know that he could have obtained it only through the proper channels; no person with flamingos so perfectly silhouetted to the road could ever be guilty of tinkerish theft. Such a species of flamingo is obvious evidence of good faith. It is also evidence of neighborliness, but the trouble is, Art's house is so remote from other houses, no one is likely to observe these plastic birds, whose lone function is to be observed.

The three of us walk into the house where Nan, Art's young wife, is nursing her baby. She is singing it to sleep, but she immediately stops when we enter the room and rises to meet us. Nan, I learn, is a Cawley, a family traditionally hostile to the Lawlesses. "Something about a horse," she says. In marrying, the two risked at least mild ostracism by their own families, and very probably the scorn of many other traveling people. Concerning which, "we just didn't give a damn, because we were both fed up with that tight way of life," says Art. Nan nods in silent agreement. She doesn't talk much. However, I notice that her dialect, which did not undergo a year's cleansing in England, is quite a bit more prominent than her husband's. She'd like to get away from tradition, but it appears that she doesn't yet have the words to do it. "A marrit woman wit' children shouldn't go up an' ax a stranger for money," she says, perhaps sounding like her mother, who she says "had t'live by beggin' from farmers."

The couch is a one-seater, and Art offers it to me, "the guest." I, in turn, offer it to Sister Margaret, who pats the cushion knowingly before sitting down. She seems to be as much at home here as the Lawlesses themselves.

Nan had been listening to the radio, and now Art shuts it off, silencing today's weather ("Clear, with patches of fog"). Then, his brow all of a sudden knitted with great seriousness, he lights a cigarette and begins talking of the things that drove him to settle here.

"The younger generation finds the road meaningless. They want to all settle. They may have seen only a little of what their parents saw, but they don't want their own children to see even *that*. Progress, you'd have to call it progress.

"I was raised in Mayo, my family came from Mayo, and it was the worst county for schooling. Man, it was! I might be only two days going to school, of a week, when the guards would come and they'd tell us we'd have to go. The guards would keep shifting us from pillar to post. We'd pull up in Castlebar, say, and a guard would be there to meet us and he'd say, 'Don't pull up here. Move on." That made it very hard.

"And then maybe you'd wake up in the morning and all the

ponies would be gone, during the night, like. You'd have to follow them by their tracks in the shit. Oh I followed them, when I was young . . .

"You couldn't even put your ponies on the road. If you did, you'd be summonsed over them; if a car hits them, you're into bother. And on the land, if you put them on the land in some farmer's field, it's trespass. What's left? Only to have them shot. . . . You see, if you think about these things long enough, you know the truth. You know that, just like that, the old life is well shot. You either die with it, or you get on a different bandwagon, as the saying goes.

"It's the parents of the itinerant people who went wrong. If they had a son, they'd want him to marry another itinerant. That doesn't let him out into the community of people. Let the girl lead him out; or let the boy go out, join the army, join some force. The older people, they'll never change because they had no education — but now the children have more intelligence than their parents because they're learning to read. Even so, it will take another two generations, the news says, before the children who are now at it, being educated, will be the same as the townspeople. I hope it doesn't take that long . . .

"The road is the best college? I spent a year in London, doing odd jobs, learning the facts of life, meeting new people, going to the odd museum, and I can tell you this, any one day of that year was more meaningful to me than all the roads in the world. ·

"Ever since I was a young lad, I wanted to be an automobile mechanic. Do you mean to tell me that you think I could have acquired any practical knowledge of that staying beside my father, who was a fine man but who was only a chimney sweep all his life? I wanted to do something more with my life than sweep chimneys. Sweeping would have no meaning for me . . .

"So you see, myself and Nan, we wanted to settle really bad."

There is a gritty conscientiousness about him that one cannot help but like, even in wishing it were seasoned with a little gaiety. He seems far too young to be entirely sober. And yet this way of presenting himself is really of a piece with his divorce from the old outlook. He aims for something new: *meaning*. A meaningful life, meaningful work, and perhaps a meaningful relationship. These are concepts of a recent vintage, and they allude to the chaos of inheritance. They assume that the world is a darkness beyond the isolated human effort; a man's birthright is no longer a place in any community. One is obliged to manufacture a meaning out of nothingness. Art's father went blind before he abandoned his work sweeping chimneys. I don't imagine that, before his loss of sight, he would have considered quitting it because he found it "meaningless." Meaning was whatever he did. And Mickey Ward, too, would never talk of a "meaningless" existence, at least until now, when he might use a different word: gaol.

Nan brings on the tea; Do I want some biscuits with it? She is solicitous to a fault. In fact, everything here is well nigh faultless. Art and Nan seem like a perfect couple; their house is spotlessly clean, and even their baby has yet to cry. Commenting on this scene, Sister Margaret's persistent smile is the facial equivalent of a Greek chorus. I begin to feel that I have been brought to a Model Home, and I begin to yearn for stronger stuff, like the pungent odor of turf burning in Tomás Walsh's inglenook. But then I realize that this sense of well-being may be no deeper than a momentary composure brought on by my visit: nobody actually lives in a Model Home. And this makes me wonder whether or not Art has been talking of a mansion he will never be able to build.

As we drive off, I give this little house a parting look. In a way, it is like millions of other houses in Dublin, Oslo, Hamburg, Istanbul, Toledo, and Sligo — except that it is sadder. For it hasn't yet been allowed to slip into the suburbs. Perhaps some day more itinerants will settle here, with more of these unobtrusive little dwellings, and in their numbers will arise a sort of auxiliary suburb.

On second thought, it may be sadder here, but it is also, for the moment, wiser. The Lawlesses have yet to worry about rising rents in their neighborhood; they have plenty of air to breathe. Their outcast status has granted them this small haven in the wilderness, where they can live more wisely than their suburban counterparts: at least they still have a sort of identity, even if it is only that of the outcast. Of course, Art would never agree to that title. Himself an outcast? Why, they even let him bring his work home from the garage.

When I return to Mickey Ward, he is standing on the steps of his caravan. He has donned a tweed cap, and has gone "out," to watch his grandchildren play. "Art Lawless is a fine lad. He can take the engine of a motorcar asunder, an' put it back together agin," he says, with very little interest in his voice. Not a particle of him moves; yet he seems remarkably alive in his musings.

Mickey's grandchildren are involved in what looks like a battlefield skirmish. Their shouts and cries are competing with a raucous swarm of jackdaws in a nearby grove.

"There'll always be somebody wanderin', that's the truth. You'll see the whole lot on the road again," Mickey suddenly says to me. Then he points to his grandchildren. "Y'see, 'twill remain. They'll break away. Even now, the young wans, six, eight, an' ten years old, they're goin' t'school, but somehow it is when they come home from school, they play ponies an' carts, an' they put down their camps, good little camps, an' the little girl goes for the firewood, or she plays at beggin', plays like she's beggin'. 'Tis there all the time. They collect tin an' iron an' brass an' cannisters. They have to do this, they have it from the parents. 'Tis like a musicianer — if you take his instrument outa his hands, he'd have t'play something else. 'Tis there inside, you can't take the music outa him. Look now."

But at the moment, these children are actually playing cowboys and Indians. Screaming a war chant with a faint brogue, one little girl tomahawks a weaponless boy with a stick passed through a potato; there's another boy with a cap pistol, and they're calling him "the Nevada Kid." A sort of log cabin has been constructed out of scrap metal . . .

"All right you lads, let's get those tinker Indians," "the Nevada Kid" is screeching. The boys are cowboys, and most of the girls are Indians. It is clearly desirable to be the former; for the Indian is the cowboy's victim.

The cinema is one of the few public places from which these children are not banned, and they've taken the format of this game from it. They like the wild life of the westerns, similar as it is to their own. The nomadism, the campfires, the wagons, the violence . . . these things they can understand. They especially like the violence, though God knows Irish history puts enough bloodshed at their disposal that they needn't have to go to America for more.

Perhaps these children are reaching out in the general direction of their own pasts. But they are escaping from Mickey (who has never seen a western), playing in fields beyond his comprehension, which has stopped comprehending, being strangely immobile now. He will remain where he is, unable to break away, and maybe tomorrow he'll spend the entire day putting a crucifixion made of straw into a bottle; his descendants have already become pioneer homesteaders in the new world.

Listenin' Was a Great Thing Once

The one who travels is storied . . .
— Peig Sayers, *An Old Woman's Reflections*

. . . the words that remain, my old story, which I've forgotten,
far from here, through the noise, into the silence, that must be
it, it's too late, perhaps it's too late . . .
— Samuel Beckett, *The Unnamable*

I DID NOT GET a story from Art Lawless for much the same reason
as I wouldn't have been able to get a Mick Jagger anecdote
from Seán Murphy. There can be no stories without fathers and
sons tilling the same hard garden, so to speak. For stories,
through the self-enclosed logic of their narrative, attest to continuity; their own, and in the lives of those who perpetuate
them. They have to do with a common ground.

Mickey Ward took many of his stories from his own father,

just as he took the trade of tinsmithing from him. This wasn't at all like "a scholar goin' t'school," Mickey states. "It was all in yerself, you had it there in yer brain. You just watched an' you listened. Listenin' was a great thing once, y'see."

But his father was a very gifted man anyway. Of *that* I can be sure. Everyone remarked upon it. When I inquire about his father's talent for stories, Mickey's answer does not appear to be in response to my particular question. Or perhaps "talent," to him, is not decided by just a lone ability. He says: "Yes, he was talented indeed. He got crippled from an accident wit' a cart an' he got hisself a crutch an' he could clear a six-foot iron gate wit' that crutch. He'd put his hand at the top, an' he'd give a spring an' shove hisself wit' the crutch that he'd get right across an' bring the crutch after him an' down under him. He would do that wit'out ever puttin' the other foot on the gate. The same way wit' a drain, when he came t'a drain. He'd look for a flat rock an' he'd give a spring off the crutch on the good leg an' he'd land right across the far side an' still have the crutch t'stop him from fallin'. There was no coddin' about it, he was great."

Perhaps this answer does, after all, disclose the truth. Perhaps crippling does help liberate the talents. Van Gogh did not cut off his ear to spite his face, he cut it off to sharpen his eye. The body learns to be resourceful when it begins to lose its parts. And when it labors in pain, it learns to be inventive. The more intense the pain, the greater the possible effect on the singing mind: the greater the song. A history of Ireland could be written in the light of that idea.

For Mickey himself, it was in the hospital that he was "brought back" — his term for remembering — to his stories. He had finally submitted himself to the devices of modern medicine after allowing "a bad scrap t'the neck I got from galvanizin'" to fester for three years. It took a while to get accustomed to an environment so different from the road. "The sky was too low," he remarks of his bed in the hospital. So he slept on the floor his first few nights there. Then came the operation ("They told me I was balanced on a scales, could ayther go up or go down, live or die"), and a protracted stay in the recovery ward. But in the crowded solitude of that ward, an odd thing happened: he began to recover stories that he thought he had lost forever.

"I don't know how it happened. The stories started comin' back t'me aisy an' free, like well-trained ponies. An' then I started tellin' them t'other patients. If there was a fellow in bed, middlin' bad, I'd get in a place where he could see me an' hear me talkin' an hear me tellin' me stories. I'd sit beside the fellow that was worrit an' sick, an' I'd tell him, we'll say, 'The Little Hairy Man of the Forest,' what I hadn't told in twenty years.

"Then I got this opinion that it was the devil's own work. 'Cause it was a hospital an' that I shouldn't be carryin' on, tellin' these stories, in a hospital. 'Twould be like a church, y'see. Well, I told this priest that it was playin' on me brain t'know was I or was I not committin' sin.

"The priest sat down beside me, an' he said, 'Yer a wonderful man.' 'I don't know,' says I. 'I'm only tryin' t'help them.' An' he says, 'That's no sin. You carry on wit' that, baycause yer doin' more for the patients than what the doctors is doin' here, an' the nurses. Yer causin' them t'laugh, people that the doctors can't get. Kape up the good work.' He put his hands on me forehead, an' said, 'You don't mind if I bless you?' 'Oh not a bit, Father,' I says. So he blessed me, an' he squeezed me head middlin' hard, an' he put the sign of the cross afterwards wit' his tongue, sayin', 'Yer a saint!' 'If I am,' says I, 'I'm a very poor wan.' "

This makes me think once again of the healing powers of the storyteller. I ask Mickey whether he agrees with the priest's notion that his stories turned him into a surrogate doctor. "Well, he says cautiously, after pausing to consider the possibility, "A manner of doctor, yes. I can go back to a time when there was a great number of storytellers an' very few doctors. Over the years, more doctors have been comin' along now. Now there isn't many storytellers at all, but the doctors, you see them the same as the grass there in it. So maybe it's true, maybe they does come from the same cloth. Only the times is diff'runt."

Then I ask him about the years before the hospital supplied

him with a truly captive audience. Did he see his storytelling in the same way in those times, too? His eyes flood me with their eagerness, and he exclaims, "I'd be often invited inta the houses of country people who wanted t'hear a good yarn, so I would. An' I loved it, I loved t'make people fonder of meself, that they'd get fond of me an' I'd get fond of them. I was able t'tell these yarns t'all classes of country people, that they'd forget about everything an' enjoy theirselves."

In the fond eyes of these country people, his stories must have made him seem better than just a tinker.

The jackdaws have flown away, and now it is only the children, continuing to play, who snipe at the silent evening with their yells. A stout woman wearing a homespun dress comes out of the nearest *tigín* and sets about making a campfire. She is Packy's wife, and she was lovely, Mickey says, when she was a girl, before the time of her own children. He doesn't think she looks so bad even now, after her sixth child. But she was once "far an' away the prettiest creature" ever brought forth by the Faulkners, her family. The Faulkners, he says, were never renowned for their attractive looks. "They were good horse trainers, though."

We return to his caravan, and Mickey immediately removes his cap, hanging it on a peg behind the door. "I could never tell a story wearin' a cap." Then he closes the sackcloth curtains and makes certain the caravan door is securely fastened. Now the others will think he's asleep and they'll be disinclined to come in and disturb him with genial cracks about joining the *Dáil*, where his "lies" could be put to better advantage. To Mickey's own way of thinking, however, the least important conclusion a man might draw from a story is whether or not it is true. Does anyone, he asks me, ever doubt that a cartwright's skill in making wheels is "true"?

He now puts in his false teeth. Words are his "racket," his son had told me earlier in the day, and he doesn't want any of them to depart his mouth muddied with imprecision. At least not now, not during a story. These teeth "will straighten out me sentences."

"Have y'ever heard 'The Fiery Dragon'?" Mickey asks me. 'Tis a yarn about giants, an' I took it from an old traveling woman, Annie Powers, when I was a chap of about sixteen years. She was very fond of the drink, an' I often gave her a pint for a story, an' I'd kape her at the wan story, feedin' her pints, until I got it, night after night . . ."

But before he can begin this story, a wild hammering rattles his door, which he opens to reveal a tearful grandchild. She stumbles in and hugs him around the knees. One of the cowboys, it seems, has stolen her "spud" and "clobbered me in the mouth with it." She swells her lips for Mickey's examination. While he is wiping off the thin trickle of blood there, she reaches for an awl he has lying on the floor, and is poised to dash out with it, to wreak vengeance on the malefactor who got her with her own weapon no less, when Mickey grabs her.

He needs the awl, he tells her, for a "tay kittle" he is making for Father O'Dee. A priest? This quiets her with extraordinary effectiveness. She puts down the awl of her own accord.

"Would you like t'hear a story, Lizzie?"

She gives him a lingering smile which her dirt-encased face only serves to enhance to the point of near rapture. Then she rushes out, returning with renewed vigor to the other children. She is too young to understand such questions. "She thought I was tellin' her to go back out an' play," Mickey explains. And he adds, "Wit' her, she's a child. But there was none of the older wans, never any of them belongin' t'me, who took any interest in stories, good, bad, or indiff'runt. My own son, if he came in an' heard me at them, off he'd go like a wild deer."

He gestures for me to turn on my tape recorder. He is determined to tell "The Fiery Dragon" now.

"There was once upon a time [his story begins] an' a very good time it was, 'twas nayther in yer time nor me own time, but it was somebody's time, when there was an old man an' an old woman, an' this old man an' this old woman was teachin' witchery an' scholarship by the l'aves of the trees. An' they had four pupils, wan from each of the four kingdoms of Ireland at that time, Munster, Leinster, Ulster, an' Connaught . . ."

A startled expression grasps his face. "Don't take that," he says, "you can't take that in, I'm tellin' it wrong. I'm tellin' 'The Little Hairy Man of the Forest' instead. They're giants in that wan, too."

And so he begins again.

"Once upon a time, an' a very good time it was, 'twas nayther in yer time nor in me time, but it was somebody's time, when there were giants once in Ireland. Now there was this giant used t'come ev'ry sev'n years t'take a girl away, any girl he'd choose, an' there was nobody could stop him. Well, there was an old man in it, an' he had a son named Jack, an' this Jack, when he came of age, left his old father's house an' wint workin' around, a farm laborer. So he wint workin' wit' this farmer, an' there was giants livin' agin him, an' these giants had a great big wall. So the farmer told Jack t'kape the cattle away from this wall. He said, 'Don't let even their breath go across the wall.' Well, the farmer had a daughter whose name was . . . her name was . . . a daughter . . ."

This time, he lets fly with a curse, and his eyes lose their concentration. They even seem to lose some of their splendid blueness.

"I've got it wrong again. I have her name forgot."

After a short silence which comes close to an apology, Mickey says, "Long ago, that's when I could best tell them. By the campfires an' the margins of the roads, well down deep in Galway. I could tell them once for six monts wit'out ever stoppin', so I could — wan time. But when yer in the wan place, an' no wan has any interest in them, an' yer not tellin' them, you just forget all about them. They l'ave yer brains, an' nayther love nor gold can bring them back."

I am very touched by all of this. The story's mortal coil has been cast off unremembered, and will anyone, anyone like Mickey, ever be able to tell it again? I feel like I'm alone here listening to the final trickle of rocks in a landslide that has made the road fully impassable; from now on, people will have to go all the way around, take the longer route, and no more stories will come directly from the mouth. Of course, one can always get "The Fiery Dragon" and its like in books of folktales or even in manuscript form in the archives of the Irish Folklore Commission. But this isn't the same. Once a story is absorbed into a book, it is divorced from its teller and it becomes like the scenario of a film, a mere outline of the real thing, neither bones nor flesh.

"What I'd like is for someone t'come up wit' a story that I have forgot, an' once he sets me on the way, like puttin' me on the right road t'where I'm goin', I'll know the right way wit' it."

Mickey's inability to read prevents him from refreshing his memory at the local library, where he probably could collect dozens of stories with ease. No, he needs human contacts, and they are not easy to find these days. He needs actual people to tell him stories. He once had these people, though sometimes at a cost: "I'd often work half a day wit' a farmer for nothing, just t'get a good story from him."

So, on a whim, I "introduce" him to a shanachie, and begin telling him a story I got from Seán Murphy, about an apprentice thief who literally steals the royal bedclothes from a king. This is the match the tinder needs, and Mickey's face toughens with the old concentration and he complains that the sequence of events is all askew, "beggin' yer pardon, but yer man is tellin' it wrong, he's left some of it out, and 'twas a landlord, not a king." He hurries to put his teeth back in again, so he can proceed down the right "road" this time. And what emerges from his mouth is indeed a story very different from Seán Murphy's, steeped as it is in the jerky rhythms of the road.

"There was once upon a time, an' a very good time it was, 'twas nayther in yer time nor in me own time, but it was some-body's time, when there was an old woman once an' she had wan son an' this son's name was Jack, a great giant of a lad. This Jack slept for twenty-wan years in bed wit'out stirrin' hand or foot, while his mother worked as a gate lodge for the landlord. Well, after these twenty-wan years, Jack stretched his feet, which knocked down the gabled end of the house. He stood up an' he knocked out the roof of the house. He got outa bed an' he shook about five stone of ashes off himself.

"Now when Jack sane what he had done, he started t't'ink, what was he goin' t'do before his mother came back. Well, he wint out an' he got a big heap of chains an' he tied them in knots together, t'make wan log chain. He pegged them on his back an' off he started t'the forest, an' when he got t'the forest, he dropped wan end of the chains an' left it, an' he came around, so he did, nearly a quarter of the forest that was in it, an' brought the rest of the chain around with him, an' when he got the two chains together, he gave a pull an' he pulled down nearly ev'ry wan of the trees. Then he stood at the trees, trim-min' an' trimmin', until he made the rafters for his mother's house. So now he wanted as much straw as would t'atch the house, an' he wint t'the haggard an' hoisted the straw on his back. There was wan end of the landlord's castle in his way, an' he didn't mane t'hit it, but didn't he hit the bundle of straw aginst the castle an' knock down part of the gable end of it that was stickin' out. Inside, the old landlord got afeared of his life, but his wife says t'him, she says, 'Wouldn't that fellow be a person ye'd feel safe wit' around the castle. You should get him, an' get rid of yer army, that wan man'll do ye, an' he better than the whole army put together.

"So Jack took a job in the landlord's castle, an' this day he was clanin', an' he came across a big gold ladle, an' he said, 'Now wouldn't that be handy t'me t'ate a bit of stirrabout off of at home, besides atin' it off of me hands, an' it's no good here.' So he took the gold ladle.

"Well, they used t'have big dinners for all the other landlords in this particular castle, an' a gold ladle was missin', an' the landlord asked Jack about it, an' Jack said, 'I sane no gold ladle, but I sane a big bright spoon an' I brought it home t'ate me stirrabout wit'.' Then the landlord got very angry, an' he said t'Jack, 'Now Jack, I took you in here t'make a good worker outa ye, I didn't take you t'make a t'ief outa you,' an' he said, 'Since t'ievery is the trade that's breakin' out in you, I'll send you off t'learn yer trade wit' t'ree professional t'iefs, an' I'll give you a year an' a day, an' if you haven't learned yer trade by then, I'll behead you, or I'll shoot you.' 'Fair enough,' says Jack.

"And so Jack wint off t'where the t'ree t'iefs lived, away from everyone, at the foot of a hill. He was wit' them t'ree monts an' they were learnin' him nothing. He was wit' them six mont's an' they were learnin' him nothing, good, bad, or indiff'runt. So this wan day there was a fair in town an' the t'iefs were talkin', they said they'd go t'the fair 'cause they were short of money. 'We'll bring ten lambs t'the fair,' they said, 'an' we'll sell them, 'cause there's no t'ievery in it at the moment.' Well, two of the t'iefs started off wit' the ten lambs, l'avin' the t'ird wit' his wife t'mind the house, an' Jack says t'this wan, 'I'll bet you a pound I'll steal the ten lambs off them wit'out their seein' me.' Your man started laughin'. 'It can't be done. Sure, it's a bet.'

"Jack wint off an' there was a shop on his way t'the town, an' didn't Jack go inta the shop an' buy a pair of shoes, an' he shortcutted across the fields an' he came out t'a place before the t'iefs was, drivin' their lambs. And the next thing was, didn't Jack put wan of the shoes down on the road in front of him, an' didn't he shit in it! An' then didn't he l'ave this shoe there on the road. The t'iefs came along anyway, an' wan of them says, 'A new shoe, an' some dirty bugger dirtied in it,' an' he t'rows it inta the ditch.

"Jack came along now, an' he came t'where there was a big wood, an' he put the second shoe on the road in front of the wood. The t'iefs soon arrived there, an' they looked at this shoe, an' wan of them said, 'There is the comrade of the shoe we're after t'rowin' in the ditch, an' now it'll be aisy washin' the dirt outa it. You stay here wit' the lambs until I come back.' 'No,' says the other fellow, 'Why should I stay? You stay until *I* come back.' So the first wan says, 'I'll tell you what we'll do. We'll tie the lambs here t'the gate, an' we'll have ourselves a race, an' whichever wan is back the first, he'll own the shoes.' Well, they did that, an' off they wint, runnin' down the road. Jack came outa the place in the wood where he was hid, an' he pegged the ten lambs across his shoulders an' back he started, t'collect his pound from the t'ird t'ief.

"Now when the two t'iefs discovered their lambs was gone, they came back an' this time, they took ten ewes wit' them t'sell, an' says Jack t'the t'ird t'ief agin, 'I'll bet you five pounds I'll take those ten ewes off them wit'out their seein' me.' 'Couldn't be done. You might cod them once, but you couldn't cod them twice,' yer man says t'him. 'It's a bet.'

"So off goes Jack agin, an' he wint back t'the wood where the two t'iefs had tied their lambs, an' when he sane them comin' along the road agin, he started shoutin', 'Ma-a-a-a!' everywhere, an' he ran here an' there, makin' 'Ma-a-a-a's!' everywhere, makin' out that there was a whole flock of lambs in it, d'you see. 'Do ye hear that?' says wan of the t'iefs t'the other. 'There's our lambs in the wood. We never wint back t'see were they there. Aren't we awful eejits?' So they tied their sheep t'the gate an' wint in t'the wood, an' when they wint in, out comes Jack an' pegged the ten sheep across his shoulder an' back he started, t'collect his five pound.

"Now Jack used t'sleep next t'the room of this t'ird t'ief an' his wife, an' the night he was after returnin' wit' these ten sheep, he happened t'overhear the t'ief an' his wife talkin'. ' 'Troth,' the t'ief says t'his wife, 'This Jack is puttin' me inta trouble wit' all

his t'ievery. I wish we could do away wit' him.' The wife says,
'Here's what you'll do then. There's a big tree outside. Tie a
rope t'the top of it, an' put a runnin' knot in it, an' put a ring in
it, about the height of a man from the ground. Put a box undernaith it, an' tell the young fellow that ye'll have a game today
wit' that rope, an' that ye'll give him ten pound t'put his neck
in that rope.'

"So the next day this t'ief told Jack that he'd like t'have a
game wit' him, an' Jack says, 'I'd love t'have a game, an' get away
from all me work here!' So the t'ief told him what he wanted
him t'do, the same as I'm just after tellin' you, an' Jack says, 'I'd
like t'see you puttin' yer head inta that first so's I can see how
'tis done.' Well, the t'ief put his head inta the rope, an' as soon
as he did, Jack pulled away the box undernaith him. That was
the end of the poor t'ief, then. Jack ran in t'the t'ief's wife, an'
he says, 'Yer man had some tricks out there, an' when I turned
away, there he was wit' his tongue hangin' out. Could be that
he's dead as mutton now.' Well, she started t'roar, but says Jack,
'You know what you'll have t'do now, you'll have t'bury him.
You'll have t'go t'the market in town an' get a shroud an' coffin,
an' then bury him. No priest will come for a man who's been
hung.' Off she goes, an' Jack wint t'where the t'ree t'iefs kept
their gold an' away he wint wit' it back t'the landlord, a rich
man now.

" 'I must have a trial of you yet, Jack,' says the landlord. 'If
you don't steal the sow an' t'ree bonhams that's in the stable
here tonight, I'll have you beheaded, or I'll have you shot.'
'That's no trouble t'me,' says Jack. 'I don't know,' says the landlord. 'There'll be two sentries in that stable, an' they'll have my
orders t'shoot anyone who tries t'pull any trickery there t'night.'
'Fair enough,' says Jack.

"Well, that night Jack wint t'a public house an' bought five
half pints of whiskey, an' he drank wan of them, an' back he
came t'the stable where the men were watchin' over the pigs.
They smelled the whiskey on him just as he was fallin' t'the

stable floor. They started t'lift him, an' says wan of them, 'By God, there's a half pint of whiskey in his pocket.' 'By God,' says the other, 'He has t'ree more half pints in his other pockets.' So they laid him back down agin, an' then started t'drink the whiskey theirselves. After a while, they got knocked out wit' the whiskey, an' Jack rose up from the floor and took the sow an' t'ree bonhams back t'the castle.

"The landlord had t'agree that Jack done his job. 'Well now, Jack,' he said, 'I have wan more for ye, an' perhaps this'll be some trouble t'you. I want you t'take the sheets that's under an' over meself an' the wife in bed this night wit'out me seein' you. I'll be sittin' in bed ready for you wit' a gun, an' I'll blast away at any bit of noise. If yer able t'take those sheets off us then,' he says, 'I'll give you me daughter in marriage an' the weight of herself in gold.' 'No trouble,' says Jack.

"Well, Jack knew of an old man that wasn't long burrit an' he wint t'the graveyard an' took this old fellow outa his coffin. He got a great big pole, too. That night he wint t'the ground bayneath the bedroom where the landlord and his wife were sleepin', an' didn't he tie the dead man onta the top of the pole an' bob him against the window, tappin' an' tappin' at it. An' as soon as he'd commenced wit' this, the landlord fired away his gun. Then Jack let the dead man fall, pole an' all.

"Now the landlord was well pleased wit' what he had done. He rushed out, an' as soon as he rushed out, Jack wint in an' got inta the bed wit' the wife, an' he kicked the sheets from under her an' over her. 'Why are you doin' that?' she says. Says Jack, 'I need t'wrap them around the body,' an' off he goes wit' them wrapped under his arm, before the landlord could get back.

"Jack returned the next morning wit' his sheets. The landlord said t'him, 'I'll have t'give you the castle now too, 'cause if I don't, you'll steal it right off me anyway, an' all I have inside it.' So he gave the castle t'Jack, an' he wint away t'Ameriky, an' we never heard from him again. Jack marrit his daughter, an' after a time, they had childer in basketfuls, they were drawin' them out in shovelfuls, the Queen of England refused t'buy them for a pence a piece. They put down the kittle an' they made the tay, an' if they don't live happy, that we may."

Well, I have gotten him to tell the story, thus proving that, unlike Antaeus, he has not altogether lost contact with his ground. He is still in touch with — which gods? Some of them, Mickey's unfailing belief to the contrary, must watch over the occasional caravan dweller, here and there. However, Mickey really doesn't need to invoke them. He doesn't need to appeal to outside help, for his words are of the same nature as himself. A poor lad with no real schooling outwits all of his masters, inheriting the earth by dint of his own canniness. One can become one's own landlord, nearly. A castle has never been available to Mickey for occupancy, but there is more geography in Ireland than there are castles to punctuate it, and he has inherited this geography, compressed it within him, and that is part of his story. By now, in fact, he may have even become his own story, since he has outlived his credibility. Or so everyone seems to think.

Every story is an autobiography, of sorts.

Before I go, Mickey offers me a cup of tea. He uses the Elizabethan pronunciation, "tay" for "tea." To hear it once is to know the eternal daintiness of "tea." This is not, with Mickey, an affectation; he never learned how to be affected. Four hundred years ago, the correct pronunciation of -ea was -ā. Inflicted with the language of their captors, the Irish retained this pronunciation even as the English, who began to consider it vulgar, slowly phased it out. The lone word the English kept was "great," as in "Grate Britain," and even that was contested in parliament, with Lord Chesterfield, who adopted the affected pronunciation (as in "Greet Britain"), remarking that only an Irishman would call it "grate."

The older traveling people continue to say "tay," among other Elizabethanisms. They don't know any better; being of a somewhat conservative nature, they tend to keep what they've been given, speaking in an alphabet of ashes. But the more educated the person, the less Shakesperean is his language. A Professor of English at Trinity College would never ask for a cup of "tay."

A campfire has now been made in the open space between the three *tigíns,* and we walk toward it. "They have ranges in their houses," says Mickey, "but still they prefer t'do their cookin' outside by the campfire. They wouldn't give that pot down there for all the ranges an' stoves in the country."

His people are all here, along with some of the Galway Mc-Donoughs.

The tea we finally drink is dark and powerful, unencumbered by milk or sugar. Traveling people traditionally drink their tea strong, Mickey says, to fortify themselves against the wet that would ease into their tents at night. Not so, the other country people, living in houses. The tea he's drunk with farmers has been usually so weak, "you could spear an eel in ten fat'oms of it, so you could."

Mickey takes some kale and potatoes from one of the pots squatting on top of the fire, and begins to eat, while his grandchildren, still at cowboys and Indians, play around him, using his seated body as a sanctuary against enemy raids.

Packy comes over and asks him for the loan of a pound, as he's going to Sligo later this evening to drink and renew old ties with the McDonoughs (Packy's wife protests that this renewal has already been going on all day.) Mickey observes that drink is good for the health, but drink taken in excess "ruins the brains." He obliges Packy with a handful of coins anyway, and then he turns to me. "Always kape a fire lit outside. When you kape a fire outside, you'll always have somebody t'come around you. But they won't come t'the house, so they won't."

I decide not to tell him that where I live a fire outside would be madness.

Body Parts

What I'd like now is to speak of the things that are left, say my good-byes, finish dying.

— Samuel Beckett, *Molloy*

Who Will You Leave Your Hands to When You Die?

> In the neolithic age, Man had already made most of the inventions which are indispensable to his security.
> — Claude Levi-Strauss, *Tristes Tropiques*

> But it doesn't do to be always looking for money. There was Whaney the miller, he was always wishing to dream of money like other people. And so he did one night, that it was hid under the millstone. So before it was hardly light he went and began to dig and dig, and he never found the money, but he dug until the mill fell down on himself.
> — a County Clare woman, quoted in Lady Gregory, *Visions and Beliefs in the West of Ireland*

> I am a good craftsman.
> — the smith Fergus MacRoy, uttered to show his fitness to raise the infant Cuchulainn

I AM GOING to Ballina, the county town of Mayo, to see a tinker friend of Mickey's with the vivid name of Felix Green. "Felix mayn't have many stories in his head," Mickey told me. "But his tin vessels are as fine as any story." In Mickey's view, the storyteller and the traditional tradesman travel the same dirt road; only the tradesman's articles are harder, more resonant on the ground than stories are. "What I wish y'could tell me, bein' an eddicated man an' all that, is why wit' all this eddication business about, they're very few good tradesmen an' story people left in the country, like?" Then, remembering Felix, who is a good tradesman, he said, "I'd know wan of that man's saucepans in heaven, so I would."

Later during the same night as Mickey's story, I sat in a Sligo pub and told a local tobacconist that part of the Ulster problem must surely come from the very idea of a city, that if people weren't compelled to crowd together like Norwegian sardines, there wouldn't be all this violence, which is like a desperate shattering of the sardine tin. I told him that in the country there is not much opportunity for people to blow each other up; or at least not as much as in the cities, where entire segments of the population can be liquidated with extraordinary ease, as Hitler proved with the Jews of Warsaw.

Almost immediately, the television above the bar proved me wrong; two members of the Royal Ulster Constabulary had just been killed, this soft evening, in the south Fermanagh country-side not too far from the border.

My tobacconist friend shook his head ("Isn't it terrible what's going on in 'the North'?"), and ordered another pint. These new killings seemed to distress him less than the new tariff that the minister of finance, in accordance with an E.E.C. mandate, had just the other day levied on cigarettes and tobacco, making it almost impossible (my friend said) "for the little man to have his smoke now." A significant mooring was going to be lost, in ordinary lives. Also, tobacco brought this man his bread, and now it didn't seem as if he would be able to sell very much of it. Would that be "the end"? he wondered.

Against his own economic dilemma, "the North" to him is like the kingdom of the past, a place where ancient hostilities take precedence over mere living. Indeed, like the past, it is a dark and unfathomable business. By the time this violence hits Sligo (if it does), it will have already merged with some baroque economic plan foisted on the country by Richie Ryan, the minis-ter of finance, in conspiratorial union with Brussels. "Sometimes I think those guns should be trained on the Dáil," my friend said to me, just before we parted.

The next day the newspapers embellished on this latest act of violence; a booby-trapped parcel had blown the two policemen literally to bits, some of which collectors with cellophane bags later found on the roof of a nearby farmhouse. One man's elbow was discovered in a turnip patch several hundred feet down the road. The other man's head was found in a hedge — the inside of the skull had been blown out and it was as hollow as an eggshell.

I thought how Mickey Ward would not have been able to read this news item. Only if someone had decided to tell him would he have learned about it. For him, it must seem like the Ulster war is being waged mostly through the media, bounding from newspaper to radio to television and back again without ever touching the ground he knows so well. He can get very little information on "the North" due to the self-containment of his caravan; along with his inability to read, he is not wired for television or radio. Yet I did not find him in frantic pursuit of this information, which after all concerns an Ireland twice removed from his own: a British Ireland, not even the middle-class Ireland that deplores the tinkers' survival. On the strength of these things, Belfast may not exist; south Fermanagh, too, might not exist. But Mickey has sent me to Ballina, which still does exist, and Felix Green, him of the palpable tinware. And moving southward now and away from Mickey, I am nonetheless heading in his direction. I am extending his mind to a sort of ravagement different than the shattered bodies in Ulster . . . to a countryside ravaged beyond the repair of peace talks and truces. It was that last news about the bomb-hollowed skull that did it. I have decided now to seek out the archaic tradesmen who lived — according to Mickey — beside the storyteller. Such men have yet to appear on the front pages of newspapers. *That,* at least, is a virtue.

South of Sligo, I happened upon the flat-cart equivalent of the elephant's burial ground, a place where these old vehicles must have come to die. It was a field with a dozen or so carts in various stages of decay, lying at grotesque bends and angles like

corpses on a battlefield. How *green* this field was! When I asked
a woman on the road about these carts, she told me that a
cartwright lived here once but "he's living in England now, or
he's dead."

But then what does one say to a cartwright these days? Elsewhere, he would have been a carpenter, and the talk would be
of prosaic things like cabinets and coffee tables. A horse-drawn
cart, however, is not a coffee table: to invoke it may require a
lost idiom.

In a way, this cartwright — whether he's dead or alive now —
was a victim of British domination as much as anyone else. For
the work possibilities, in a backward country, are necessarily
backward. Being a land of cheap labor, Ireland represented a
threat to British industry for the longest time and successive
British regimes seldom had any qualms about checking the development of Irish industry. Which meant that Ireland was kept
at the pre-industrial stage well into the present century. All that
remained to a man was to turn this underdevelopment into
something rich and strange. Thus when Mickey Ward discussed
his own handiwork with me, his eyes moved with a sparkle not
to be found, say, within the confines of a British Leyland Motors
factory. This sparkle, like an I.R.A. bomb, is the vengeance of
the past.

But it is nearly all in the eyes now. The rest is bits and pieces,
outmoded bodies, functionless hands. It is the end and from the
end of a world there at least emerges a certain kind of queer
poetry, a lost idiom. So what follows are my notes on meeting
those tradesmen who can still be found — notes and fragments
only, like pieces of a body.

I find Felix Green in a neighborhood of row houses stretching westward. He and his large family relocated here five years ago from a wattle tent that saw action on a variety of western fronts. He is a man of about fifty-five, with teeth that resemble two rows of miniature slanting dolmens. Stationary life seems to agree with him, except on Sunday afternoons, which he spends drinking with old acquaintances "still on the tramp." "Drink always brings me back again," he tells me.

The first thing I ask Felix is whether he has any stories. He thinks for a moment, then admits he has a "good wan." Do I know what Mayo men sent down rabbit holes before ferrets hit the country? Answer: the Galway man.

Well, it certainly is a "story." I tell him that I've heard the same story told in Cork at the expense of the Kerryman; and in Limerick, on the man from Clare. It seems that for backwardness, the scapegoat is always the next county over; just as, in the rest of Europe, venereal disease is invariably the disease of the next country.

Felix replies that he's also heard this story told at the expense of the tinkers, "all t'rough the West."

Felix still isn't too sure of the purpose behind my visit. He shows me his arthritic hands and says, "You get so many of us people wit' art'ritis baycause we sit down in the dampness an' make cans." Finally, he warns me: "Tin isn't the best trade to go in for at the moment. 'Tis all plastic an' aluminium now — the aluminium, particular, took everything out of our hands. An' the tin you'll buy is like tissue paper — it'll open before you have the can rounded at all. 'Tis just colored now, more iron now, an'

the iron rusts. Even wit' that, it's thirty-five pounds a case."
And: "There was never any profit outa tin. You won't work for
money, only just t'survive. An' be sure of this, that you barter
whenever you can — t'ree or four pounds of horsehair will stand
you better than a half crown for the work you put inta a bucket."

But when I tell him that I'm not planning to set myself up at
his trade, he looks disappointed. Had he assumed that I was a
ray of hope for this otherwise dying profession? In retrospect,
he seemed to be apprising me of the hard facts first, before
moving on to the glories of the trade. He tells me, "I enjoyed
makin' cans more than anything else I sane in my day."

Enjoy*ed*? Making cans does remain his trade still, doesn't it?
Yes, but he observes that it is no longer crucial to the community like it once was; that now, in fact, it is mostly a tourist
trade, with most of his sales going to summer visitors from
England and America, who somehow manage to locate the
shops where he wholesales his wares. "The price of tin bein'
what it is, the only lad who can afford it now is the tourist," he
says, and adds with some bitterness, though under his breath,
"An' yer own people wit' hardly enough t'kape them in fags."

Felix brings out some of his work. Plain vessels, they are:
funnels, delph, porringers, saucepans, buckets, pannikins, and a
lawn lantern, a variation on the lanterns once used by tinkers on
their carts when they had to traverse a road at night. This last
item is the most popular of them all with the tourists. Mounted
on a pole, it provides just the right illumination for a suburban
lawn at night.

These articles have leaped from merest functionality to the
status of antiques without even undergoing the dignity of a slow
decline. But as antiques, they are also austerities, with no ex-
terior designing or quirks of style, with nothing to recommend
them but their native obsolescence.

"So I'll know it's my own if ever I come across it agin, I
sometimes puts a little shamrock on my vessels," says Felix. He
has accorded them the perfect emblem.

The less outgoing the object, the more personality it would seem to have. That idea is confirmed by Charlie Cawley, who was once a blacksmith in the west Mayo village of Belmullet. "There wouldn't be a horseshoe in any part of the county but I'd know who made it," he says. "If you're used to a person's handwriting . . . well, I know the horseshoe in the same way. Oh, I almost forgot. I knew two brothers in Crossmolina, blacksmiths once, and you couldn't tell the difference between either of their shoes. They were the only ones."

The Mayo cooper Maurice Moran had written poems in his youth describing his satisfaction at making barrels, "but they're lost now, I believe, those poems." It is a wonder that he wrote them at all, barrels are such plain, unlyrical manifestations from the hands. But in these creations of wood and metal, he must have recognized a being of his own humor. " 'Twas something in me, I guess, like milk from a cow."

Kiltoom, County Roscommon: I ask John Kenney what trades he knew.

"I was a professional rabbit-trapper in my time, and made a very good living at it," he says, and then passes me a poem he's just written excoriating the use of myxomatosis, "the myxy," to liquidate rabbits ("Man's ignorance I recall,/He destroyed the lovely creature that provided food for all . . ." it begins). "And then I was a basket maker as well. If the day was well, I'd go halfway with baskets and still go for rabbits. If time was left over, I'd write a poem."

"I always kept the door to my forge wide open," says the blacksmith. "'Twasn't just for the horses, you see, but for the people too, that they'd be drawn together."

Time and again, it has been asserted that those who stayed at home did so because they lacked (perilous word!) initiative; that only "the dregs of the chromosome pool," the softest and the least intelligent, could not bring themselves to seek their fortunes in Glasgow or in Boston; but, in fact, the "initiative" of many who remained at home takes the form of classical restraint, as in the old Gaelic songs that achieve their lovely effects through holding back the emotions. For such people, the street noises of Glasgow were less sane sounds than the rhythms of a smith's sledge against his iron.

Its people say that the parish of Kilbaha is the most depopulated in the whole of Clare. They *insist* on it; from where else would their sense of themselves as survivors come? It is the continuity of loss that seems to matter to them, as though it were not loss but love that had molded their lives.

"Is there a blacksmith living near here?" I inquire of a man who is herding his sheep across the road near Kilbaha village.

"No, there's none," he replies. "The last one, Peter McNamara, moved away ten years ago, himself and his four brothers that had the trade. But I could shoe your horse if you need to have it shod."

He glances back down the road, expecting to see my horse.

Jimmy Lowell, of Ennistymon, County Clare, is a farrier retired into simple electric-welding. Nowadays, he earns his bread repairing parts for tractors and motorcars, but "Sure, anybody can do that. You can do that yourself, with just a bit of practice. But you wouldn't do the horseshoeing now, that's for sure."

Jimmy is approaching sixty years of age; still comparatively young, as farriers go; older, as mechanics and welders go. His father shod horses until his mid-seventies, when he took the easier job, a farrier's former privilege, of pulling human teeth. His father never hurt for horses; neither did Jimmy, up until about ten years ago. There'd always be horses waiting outside his forge, "fourteen, sixteen, eighteen and twenty pairs of shoes of a market day in this town. Today, it's all tractors. It's progress, that's what they tell us. And maybe it is."

He glows when he discusses the excellence demanded by his trade. Yes, it was sweat work; no, he didn't mind it at all — except, sometimes, when he had to shoe a remarkably "contrary" donkey. His snappy, vigorous style of speech betrays a compulsion that must have stood him well in his forge, of a market day.

"The farrier trade has gone on over two hundred years in my family. I acquired it by staying beside my father. I'd be always watching him, you see, and if I wouldn't be watching him, I'd get a 'dart' — to make sure I was watching. Eventually after that I was let to take off a shoe. That's all he'd let me do is take off a shoe. In another two years, he let me clean a hoof. After that, he let me fit the shoe. There was twelve months of that business, and then he let me nail the shoe, but he put two nails in first to keep the shoe in position. There were six more nails to drive. He watched me carefully. If the shoe moved, back or over, he was right beside me, to give me a nudge and get it into position again. Finally, I nailed my first shoe.

"There's more brain work in driving one nail than they use in driving a motorcar. You're driving between life and death, see, because there's not a big lot in some hoofs between the horn and the flesh inside the hoof. You may learn to drive a motorcar in five or six or ten lessons, but you won't make a horseshoe, clean a horse's hoof and shoe it properly, in three years of practice. I drove my first horseshoe when I was sixteen years of age. Years later, I could still make a mistake — but I wouldn't make many, because the horse would always be there, telling me if I'd be making any little blunder at all. How would a motorcar ever tell you that, now?

"Today, the technical school is training them to shoe only the racehorses, and that does away with the trade. There's no young fellow going to serve his time with a blacksmith, since he's going to be kicked around with horses. He'll never be able to get down to the practical work, though. You see, theory is no good. You get a contrary horse, and he'd run to the next county. You'd want to get down to the experience of every type of animal. I shod horses from all over, and I'd always know what a horse was going to do, was he going to pull me, or was he going to drag me, or was he going to lash out with a kick. I guarantee you none of those fellows would be able to shoe an ass, 'tis the most difficult animal you ever shod.

"This trade was once an art in itself. I have a certificate to that effect from the Department of Education which I got back in 1932. Once, you'd love to see a horse newly shod. I felt proud of shoeing a horse. I could take a raw piece of iron, turn it down into a horseshoe, take the horse's hoof and put that shoe on, and — 'tis like magic, isn't it? — that horse could walk away in comfort. One man said to me, 'I saw them crawling in to you, and they came out walking. You must have given them legs.' That's it, so I say. I am an artist, or I was, and the horse was in it, anyway."

Then the horse was — his Muse? That is too fastidious a word for a farrier. Whatever the source of Jimmy's inspiration, though, the gears of tractors do not stimulate it, and he is stuck with a routine as dismal, to him, as farrier work would have been to James Joyce.

A trace of incredulity lurks in Jimmy Lowell's voice when he informs me, "I met English people, and they never saw a horse shod in their life. What were they doing with theirselves all the time?"

There is a plenitude of ample, big-boned men in west Clare, perhaps to make up for the space where there are no men at all. People around Kilkee call the cartwright Pat Cloghessy "Pat the Hill" because he is immense even for this region. When he walks, they say it is the shifting of land masses. His broad face looks as though it has been hewn from a vast cabbage. But he is an unusually quiet man, whose melancholic disposition does not seem to be related to the decease of his trade.

Pat has worked in the same scarred, dust-moted shed since 1939; he purchased it for a pittance from another cartwright who believed that it had become a haven for "fairies." Pat says that he hasn't heard, seen, or in any way experienced "fairies" these thirty-six years. "I guess they took their trade where there'd be more call for it," he says ever so softly. From his tone, I gather he's made that observation before.

Like Jimmy Lowell, Pat talks keenly about those aspects of his trade that involve the hands, and alludes to his first wheel as if it meant growing to adulthood: "When I was fifteen, my father took sick and I made this wheel, for a donkey trap. The man I made it for thought it was a very good job and said, 'Who will you leave your hands to when you die?' It was a wooden wheel, with iron shod. It was no trouble to me, and after I had it made, I thought I was the happiest lad in the world. Right then, I was following in my father's footsteps. I was a man then."

Seated on a large vise, Pat is smoking a Woodbine. All around him, like detached bones, is the gallimaufry of his existence: half-ruined and half-repaired and never-to-be-repaired wheels, a set of Conestoga wagon wheels for a "western" pub, wheel-barrows, and the nearly completed body of a box cart he is making for a retired Galway businessman who owns no horses ("He wants it for his grandchildren, to say that they had once seen a genuine box cart and maybe played in it").

What does one say to a cartwright? Thinking about what Jimmy Lowell had said about himself, I ask Pat if he considers himself an artist, and he looks puzzled for a moment, before answering, "Oh yes, that too." But scarcely anyone, these days, drops in to commission a new work from him (his wheels are twenty-two pounds the set). Thus, he earns his wages by doing carpentry — making cribs and coffins, a fit combination.

"It was once considered a good week's work to make a set of wheels. But no more, I don't see no point to it no more."

(This triple negative flashes out from his usually correct speech like a knife just unsheathed. The point, it seems, can only be made by dropping the pretense of grammar.)

"I don't make them anymore. I just repair them, just repair the odd one, like the one I'm doing now. At the moment, I have seven or eight wheels to shoe, and some of them have been here for months. The men keep coming in for them, and I keep telling them, 'Next week, next week.' But I'm afraid it will be never. It takes too much fuel to light a fire, and with the cost of fuel today, well . . . I'd get more doing any kind of work, for anyone, than I'd get for myself making wheels. I get more for coffins, now, than ever I got for wheels. And as you know, there'll always be someone in need of a coffin.

"I have four sons. It'd be nice to have one of them able to make a wheel. It might be something he'd appreciate, though I wouldn't dream of him earning a living at it. I'd like him to be able to say he could make a wheel, and maybe — maybe he will make one."

Later on, when I ask one of Pat's sons if he'd like to make a wheel, he looks at me as if he had seen a ghost.

In contrast with Pat, Michael O'Halloran, a Galway cart-wright, is short and rawboned, as slender as a blackthorn branch, and it's a mystery to his friends that he's alive at all — his closest neighbor has never, in fact, seen him in the act of eating so much as a single potato. Michael admits that he has lost his taste for food. He believes this happened during his apprentice years, when his metabolism switched from a need for conventional fare to a need to make donkey carts: "When I first began the trade, I had enough food all right, but 'tis a peculiar thing about a man when he's placed in a predicament like that, he goes off his food, he doesn't want his food. His whole mind is set in his work, with the result that he has his whole appetite taken away. I never knew I wasn't eating, and still I was healthy. And I'm healthy yet."

A singular item: that the motions of labor, for this man, are both less and more than a dance of bread.

The terms "worker" and "working class" imply an army of like-minded persons, all directing themselves to a single common end. Whether processing food or constructing Volkswagens, that end is pretty much the same everywhere. *Something* had to be done to keep an increasing sprawl of humanity occupied, and so it was put to work producing items of a curious redundancy.

" 'The workers' are dissatisfied with their wages, Mr. Pringle."

"Well, we'll have to satisfy their demands, else we won't be able to reach our quota of birdbaths this year."

I'm finding men who are not, were not, "workers," in the Marxian sense. Capital was not their gain; the ends of their work were absorbed entirely into the work itself, which joined with the work of other men, in other trades and in the fields. These men remained themselves; and in their communities, their "class" was determined by the degree of richness in their personalities. The steam hooter's call never awakened them in the morning. If it had, how would they have been able to remain "witty." For, as Mickey Ward told me, "All tradesmen do be witty."

Now I know exactly what to say to a cartwright.

Michael O'Halloran has just finished reading this week's *News of the World*, and he comments that Jackie cuckolded John Kennedy at least three times while he was in office, once with former vice-president Richard Nixon.

"That probably isn't true" is the lone thing left to say.

In some quarters, truth is of necessity the handmaiden of fiction and fiction the handmaiden of tourism. The brochure for *Rent-an-Irish-Cottage, Ltd.* is a bit uneasy about visitors getting the wrong idea: "We're not asking you to rough it; to go uncomfortably back to nature. We're not putting you down in the middle of a wilderness that's strictly for the birds. We're inviting you to step back a century and live in a typical Irish thatched cottage, complete with half door, open fireplace, traditional furnishing — but also endowed with all the modern conveniences [i.e., flush toilets] that make life more liveable." So far, eleven "villages" of such houses have been manufactured by *Rent-a-Cottage* and more are on the way, all "within easy distance of Shannon International Airport." From this last bit of information, it can be seen that the architects of these facsimile rural villages have the international traveler in mind: a little piece of leprechaunish charm right by the airport, begorra, before the visitor hits the Sistine Chapel and the Acropolis.

In Carrigaholt, west Clare, John Ledwith is perched on the roof of a *Rent-a-Cottage*, thatching it. It has been a mere three years since he last thatched this same roof. "In the days when I was thatching up and down the country here," he tells me, "a good coat of thatch would last nearly fifteen or twenty years. Now three years finishes it, because it goes through the mill and the straw is all broken and it takes the wet then. The flail was better. It didn't bend the straw all over, only where the grain was, and the barley wasn't flattened out. The flail was better all right, but no man knows how to use one now. They can't take them in their hands."

Yet John isn't at all annoyed at having to put in a repeat performance with this roof. "These houses are the first thatching work I've done in over fifteen years, the first work, continual like," he says. *He* is real; it's just that the garden around him is imaginary.

After he's climbed down his ladder, I ask John if he voted to join the Common Market in 1972, and he replies, No, what has the Common Market ever done for thatchers, that he should want to vote for it? He is joking, of course. But he has no alternative now except to joke. Tradesmen are supposed to be witty.

"Thatching is a thirsty old trade," John Ledwith comments, and then suggests that we adjourn to the local pub. As we walk there, a strong wind drives the grass and heather crouching to the ground. We arrive just in time to beat a wild downpour of rain. Soon an Irish-American visitor (no doubt interrupted in the hot pursuit of his genealogy) edges over to us and complains, "It always rains when I come to Ireland." Then he stands back and waits for an answer to what is obviously an accusation. Finally, John says, "Yes, mister. But it rains when you do not come, too." For he himself accepts the rain and bad weather with a sense of superiority, as to fate.

The cockleshell curragh doesn't brave the elements, it *is* the elements. When it crosses the sea, it becomes the sea itself, and one doesn't feel the human intercession of tar, sailcloth, and timber so much as the force of the waves rearing up under them, effacing them. The aboriginal curragh-maker, perhaps taken with the sea, may have intended this effect, wherein the body itself seems to be ploughing over waves and falling into troughs; thus, he made his boat delicate yet strong.

"I'd sooner trust myself in one of my 'canoes' than in a boat the size of the *Titanic*," says Brendan O'Daly, of Dingle, a curragh maker.

Brendan shifts his sensitivity naturally from boats to fiddles, which he also makes. "I could start right now at making ye a fiddle, but it'd take the year nearly before I could have it complete and done — that is, if you wanted a good one." Two subtle skills, different yet also the same. "A fine 'canoe' dances on the water in every kind of weather," says Brendan. Like the movement of a fiddle bow, like dancing to a fiddle.

Cahir O'Doherty and his Dazzle Band, Tony and the Western Union, Hugh Keleghan and Delta Dawn, Liam Byrne and his Kentuckey Five, Shaun O'Down and Ding-a-ling, Ray Lynam and the Hillbillies, The Singing O'Sullivans, Brian Harkin and the Plainsmen, Gene Stuart and the Homesteaders, Bill Ryan and Buckshot, Brose Walsh and the Rockaways, The Alamoes, The Kilmovee All-Rounders, The Rustlers, The Clare Cowboys, Brian Coll and the Buckaroos, Killarney's Swinging Jarveys, Christie and the Blarney, Philomena and Rambling Men, Larry and the Country Roads, The O'Brien Outlaws, Pat Ely and the Storytellers, Brendan Quinn and the Mighty Avons, Brendan Bowyer and Big 8, Anne and the Swinging Marines, The Sensational Dixies, The Smoky Mountain Ramblers, The Astronauts, The Red River Valley Boys, June and the New Smokies, The Round Towers, and Frankie McBride and the Polkadots.

And so goes the confusion of one west with another. These popular Irish bands have stopped at Nashville on their way to the hotel bar, and as a result, they probably didn't have the time to make their own instruments, or their own minibuses.

"What is the world to a woman if her husband wants to sit down today and make barrels?" the west Kerry cooper asks me.

His family is well-known locally for its Republican sympathies. In fact, he says that his son, a construction worker in England, was recently picked up for a "possible" I.R.A. connection; was jailed, interrogated, and released; and went back to raising girders on the same sort of high rise where he himself lives — perhaps (his father winks) making the occasional bomb on the side. Though I haven't met the son, I agree that he may still be "at bombs": barrels do not conform nearly so well to high-rise decor.

The young, unoccupied tinker loves to hunt rabbits. "I'm a terrible man for hunting. I hunt morning and night, and if you want the truth, I don't care about rabbits. For all the rabbits I've caught and killed, I never ate a bit of one. If I brought one home, I'd give it to somebody." The odd man out, seated on the lowest rung of the social ladder, lower even than his father, and having no prideful use to which he can put his hands, he must exert domination over something, preferably something living.

A Catholic milkman has been shot in Springmartin Estate, and other milkmen in west Belfast have just suspended deliveries in protest.

On a road in Clare, a farmer approaches me in a donkey cart filled with churns of milk he is delivering to the local creamery. He pulls up beside me to ask if I'd like a ride. But once I've boarded the cart, it doesn't move. The farmer explains: this donkey is young and a little contrary and he isn't too accustomed to passengers.

Does the pig gelder become a physician specializing in skin ailments? No, mercifully; no one was around during Jack Hanrahan's youth to plan his future with that kind of Germanic efficiency. No one in those days ever assumed that the trade of Jack's father wouldn't last his son at least a lifetime. But now far fewer farmers are keeping pigs, and "Jack the Knife," as he was once called, is spending his last years before the old-age pension cleaning the litter from streets in Limerick city. "A dirty job, but it pays better than 'treating' pigs," he says. "'Tisn't as interesting, though."

The mauve, holiday-making Scotsman enters the hotel bar in Clare for a little fastidious boozing. His somewhat mincing manner identifies his clan instantly (daring not to speak its name, he shouts it from the rooftops). He is distinctly a rara avis in a "townland" where people have always bred their own — when they've bred at all — without any specialized knowledge of the alternatives.

Right away a few of the lads begin codding the man on the subject of alien sexual methodologies, and he takes it all affably, even standing the bar to a round of drinks. After he's left, the thatcher I'm talking to bends over in my direction and says in a low, hushed voice, "I'm seventy years old, and it's only just now I've learned that over there in Scotland, men do be going up other men's arses."

Naïve, perhaps (he himself might find an ignorance of thatching techniques even more naïve). But this unmarried thatcher worked at innocent altitudes, fifteen and twenty feet closer to the heavens than other people; and he was beyond the imagining of *any* sexual love there.

"Did you ever talk to any rat charmers?" asks the bog man while piling his turf into a neat trapezoid. "That was a great profession here once. There was a man here and his name was Krogher Highe and he was a rat charmer of great ability. He could bring a plague of rats to you, or take them from you. He was a terrible man for the liquor, and one day he went into the village of Feakle and asked the woman attending the bar to fill him a pint of stout. So she filled it, but he had only a coupla pence in his pocket. 'You haven't it all there,' she said. 'I can't give it to you.' And she pitched it out back again to the barrel.

'Well, I'll tell you,' says he, 'when I call again, you'll give it to me.' And so he went away. That night the woman woke up to discover the house was — all rats! They were climbing in the bed with her, even — all over the place, up where the sugar was, where the meat was. Well, she run on to where Krogher's house was in her horse and trap, at four in the morning. 'Didn't I tell you?' says he. 'I'll give you a whole barrel of it,' says she, 'if you'll only come and clear the rats.' And so he called the rats away then, very quick, like.

"That's all done away with now, they're just a handful of rat charmers left in this country now."

Nothing to live for? The old weaver sets down his pint and gives a surprisingly wide-mouthed and husky laugh. There's always the joy of a good pint, and there's also the first cuckoo in spring ("'Tis an altogether different song she sings from the rest"). Separate or together, at least *those* are two things.

Wherever Peter Joe Quilligan, this cuckoo-discerning weaver, travels, he is invariably called back to a near-legendary doss house kept by Bobby Graves (no relation to the poet, or anyone else, "I never had no family, all my life, never") for erstwhile tradesmen down and out in Sligo. Around town, Mr. Graves's establishment is known as The Tippler's Rest, and its charm lies

in its resolute lack of charm. Its habitués would have it no other
way; they seem to respect a lodging house that contains traces
of nearly everybody who ever lodged there, as The Tipplers'
Rest does. Ragged furniture, Rorschach drink-smears, stained
beds, tobacco leavings, some tradesman's abandoned adz —
such are this inn's enticements. Along with Mr. Graves's sym-
pathy for the man who has seen better days.

"I was a lodger here once myself. The old woman who had it
before me went feeble, and she fell down the stairs, the blood
came out her ears and out her mouth, and she was put up in the
hospital. Now a blacksmith who'd been here many times said I
would be the best to take it over, because I don't go out much,
very seldom — my legs are weak and I have to carry two sticks
to travel. So I've had it for the last fifteen years, and I have no
complaints.

"Every class of tradesman comes here, that'd be down and
out. Broken-down tradesmen, tradesmen that drank, the traveling trades were very often the trades that stayed with me. Some
of them would be tailors and stonecutters, some of them would
be blacksmiths. They'd come for a night or two or three and
then go again. Some of them would be farm laborers and they'd
wait a week till they could get a job, fitted in with a farmer.
They came from every county here. For you see, they'd be
lodging here and they'd go out and meet their comrade, a
Knight of the Road, and they'd tell him about it. 'Twasn't a
Knight of the Road that ever traveled the road but was here —
every class, good and bad, was here.

"Oh yes, they pay me a few shillings, but when they don't
have any money, I won't see them out. If a man comes in drunk,
I'll keep him all the same. If he's down and out, I won't see him
sleeping out — 'twould only make it worse for him. When I
have a bed up there, there's no good in having it empty and a
man outside without one. For you see, some of them comes
here, and they don't have a penny. They don't have a bit of grub
or nothing, so I gives them a sup of tea and a bed, the best I can
do for them. I wouldn't like to meet a man out on their own, out

in the rain, with no place to go, no work, no nothing. I know the meaning of that, myself.

"The man that was in it originally — even before the old woman — he was a sweep, and he saved up enough money for to buy this house for five pounds. 'Twas only a thatched house of one floor at that time, and he put slates on it, added another floor to it. The man that was next to him had a lower house, of just one floor, and he brought the sweep to court for raising his house higher than his own. Couldn't he raise his house high as he liked? your man asked in court."

What will happen to this house when he himself can no longer look after it?

"I expect the County Council will tear it down."

Even while I'm talking to him, there is a knock at the door. He hobbles very, very slowly to see who it is. After all, he has plenty of time. Finally, he opens the door and standing there at the threshold is a priest, with a short, shabby man obviously deep in his cups.

"This fellow was once a cartwright, Mr. Graves," the priest says.

After Me, It'll Be Dead.
Poetry, I Mean

What life like that of the bard can be, —
The wandering bard, who roams as free
As the mountain lark that o'er him sings,
And like that lark a music brings
Within him, where'er he comes or goes, —
A fount that for ever flows!
— Thomas Moore, "The Wandering Bard"

. . . imagination's such a torture that you can't bear it without whiskey.
— Larry Doyle, in G. B. Shaw: *John Bull's Other Island*

ASLEEP IN HIMSELF, stretched out on a bed in one of Mr. Graves's upstairs rooms, is Anthony Fergus. "A motorcar ran over his foot," says Mr. Graves. "'Twas a North of Ireland plate, but he doesn't know enough about motorcars to know the make of it. He had a few pints on him at the time, and he must have been walking in the middle of the street."

Hearing himself discussed, Anthony descends the stairs, his left foot swathed in towels and the *Irish Independent*. From beneath a black Stetson hat, which time has flattened into a near-beret, his gray-blond hair droops like unwashed fleece. His teeth are yellow and broken, like those of an old horse. And red spiderwebs cling to his cheeks; their intricate patterns illustrate his fondness for drink.

Anthony is eager to put the story right as to the precise nature of his accident. His hands flutter in front of his face like a pair of birds as he talks. It seems that he was taking the bus from Ballycastle (near where he makes his home) to Sligo for the funeral of his sister, a nun, and because he had taken drink, he had gotten off at Ballysodare, thinking it was Sligo, though he had been in Sligo dozens of times, and once he realized his mistake, he proceeded to travel the remaining five miles to Sligo on foot, in a state of mild mourning. Almost there, he was walking on the margin of the road, and a lorry driver stopped to ask him the whereabouts of the turnoff to Ballymote ("Do you know that song, 'Old Ballymote'?" he interjects. "It goes this way — 'In County Roscommon through hailstones and rain,/I was crossing the fields on my way to the train . . .'"), and after walking up to tell him, he must have continued on in the middle of the road, for the next thing was, a motorcar with a Northern license had come and gone, mashing his foot in the process.

"That is the manner of story," he concludes, "that Homer would probably be opening up his ears to."

Homer, where has he heard of Homer?

"Just before it, I was sitting on the bus, and I was sitting next to a young novitiate priest, and he was reading one of Homer's books. He tells me what, that this Homer is the greatest poet afield and afoot. Do you know now, is this Homer living at present? Because if he is, I'd like to swap poems, some of my own poems, with him."

Anthony has decided not to attend his sister's funeral; he'd feel too gauche now, with the *Independent* wrapped around his foot by a hay rope. Also, being a proud man in the matter of religion, so he explains, he wouldn't want the nuns to see him "big with drink." Would he like to see a doctor about his foot, then? No, he just wants to go back to Ballycastle now. I accept his invitation to drive him back.

After he has clambered into the car with a tipsy indeterminacy of movement, he begins to shrug off his accident: "I am more fortunate than the Kennedys, because I'm alive and those poor people are dead, because they had too much money. If they were just living something like myself, they would have been alive today. If they had done that, nobody would watch them to kill them. They were all killed as young men, and I don't think that they had committed a crime. They should have gone back to where they started before it was too late. You get my point? I am luckier than the lot of them, because I've just got the one foot a bit wounded."

He is truly Ptolemaic in these pronouncements; all global events are shrunk to his own size, where they can be dispatched with the same ease as a pint of stout. Hermetically sealed off from the rest of the world, he can define his limits where he pleases, which he does, and no one will know the difference — least of all, himself. Hence, he adopts this tone of familiarity with the rich and the famous; they are just extensions of himself, and he has never asked of himself, Am I enough?

But, as with the features of certain animals on the brink of extinction, some of Anthony's personal traits have developed to a fantastic degree. The great Irish elk grew antlers so large they were unsupportable; Anthony's own extravagance, as befits a man who often calls himself "The Last of the Bards," consists in his not being able to control his poetry — if poetry it is. In that sense, he is all antlers. A good many things draw him back to some shadowy bardic notion of himself. Even as the car passes a boggy skein of lakes black as death-tarns, typical north Mayo land, he abruptly bursts into song:

> I wish I was by that dim Lake,
> Where sinful souls their farewell take
> Of this vain world, and half-way lie

In death's cold shadow, ere they die.
There, there, far from thee,
Deceitful world, my home should be:
Where, come what might of blood and pain,
False hope should ne'er deceive again.

That is Thomas Moore, and Anthony goes a trifle soft when his name is mentioned.

Actually, Anthony juggles his self-appointed titles somewhat promiscuously. One day, he's "The Last of the Bards," the next day he'll be "The Last of the Minstrel Boys," and then on another day, he might be "The Last of the Wandering Minstrels." One thing is constant: he is preoccupied with his own lastness. Will there ever be another like him, "at least in this part of Mayo"? He is fairly convinced that there won't be, and this elicits from his lips a bold lament: "After me, it'll be dead. Poetry, I mean. They'll never know it again in this country. It's all money now, money, money, money. Money and tablets and land speculation."

He uses this same high heroic tone to suggest "a few jars" when we come to a pub on the side of the road. He hasn't any of "this money" on him at the moment — would I mind buying him a jorum of drink? Anthony won't beg for what instinct tells him is his right. He won't become whiny and accommodating; instead, he puts both his hands on the steering wheel when the car shows no sign of stopping.

Nowadays, Anthony's bardic activities are limited to the songs and recitations he performs in local pubs for drink. Many of these are of his own devising. "I've made up hundreds on top of hundreds of songs and verses and all that stuff, and sometimes I fit them to old airs, and sometimes I don't. Take a verse like

Your journey here is short, my man,
It climbs up to the stars,
And the road where Saint Peter stands,
It has no motorcars.

"You could hardly improve that by putting music on it, or at least, that's my opinion."

In these pubs, he is just barely tolerated, and his prospective audiences often buy him his "jars" if he'll promise to be quiet, an offer he is quick to take. Thirty years ago he could lay more claim to his honorific titles; in those days, he traveled from town to town in Mayo, Sligo, and Leitrim, singing in the streets for a few shillings and playing his concertina. Fair days, he says, were the only days he had enough money for "great boozing." Yet he drank much less in those days, too. And he seems to have been more widely tolerated as well.

"I had 'stage-houses,' friends who'd put me up and feed me, like Mr. Graves; he was only one of many. Grand friends who'd appreciate what I was doing, the life that I was leading. A hard life. The traveling musician and the poet man couldn't make a living at it, he just kept going, kept going. I had an old concertina I used to play, but in the end, there was no keys in it, and I'd be pulling it in and out, and there was no notes, only nonsense. So I had to stop."

To be the "last" of the bards implies an unbroken line of them, and at least in his own family, Anthony cannot even trace it back as far as his own father, "a small farmer and nothing else, never making anything of himself. Only he drank a lot, and I suppose you could say I got that from him. His drinking made for some good cracks, man. Once he was stumbling down the road to Ballygrady in a terrible way, and this priest, a Father Quinn, walks up to him and says, 'You're drunk again,' and my father says, 'So am I, Father.' He was in such a bad way, he thought the priest was after saying that *he* was drunk! In the end, 'twas drink what killed him. He was eighty or thereabouts.

"My own idea is, the whole business just rose up in me like the furze that does be in the fields. Now!'"

This "idea" he tosses off with a cavalier nod of his head. But maybe, he does suggest, it goes all the way back to the *very* old times, to the old kings and clan leaders, to the time when minstrels and bards and gleemen wandered "our four green fields" and when some nobleman would have been proud to be patron to men like himself. It is too much! Anthony can only celebrate this possibility by breaking into song, Thomas Moore again;

> Let Erin remember the days of old
> Ere her faithless sons betray'd her;
> When Malachi wore the collar of gold,
> Which he won from her proud invader,
> When her kings, with standard of green unfurl'd
> Led the Red-Branch Knights to danger; —
> Ere the emerald gem of the western world
> Was set in the crown of a stranger.

Listening to him sing these lines, I think: Perhaps he *is* the last of the wandering bards, the last voice out of a tradition that has turned lush with eccentricity in its final stages and now has gone on one last spree before joining the great cattle drive to uniformity. Perhaps tradition, as it lies dying, becomes a voluble crank. In nearly everyone's view, Anthony has gone to bits and pieces with his craving for drink and his various obsessions. Yet wandering back and forth inside his own enchanted vacuum, he may be all that's left now. The other Minstrel Boys to the wars have gone.

Anthony's own attitude toward tradition is at the very least paradoxical. On the one hand, he likes to think that he is very much a part of it; on the other, he invokes Moore's *Irish Melodies* — slight Anglo-Irish stuff, really — as though they were Columbkille's Prophecies. He has never heard of Owen Roe O'Sullivan; likewise, he is a stranger to the Irish language, which he calls "that eejit tongue." And when I ask him if he can sing any song in Irish, he fulminates against the very idea of it: "Damn the Irish language! I don't want to hear the Irish language, let alone sing it. Leave everybody to theirselves, that's the way God left them. A language is no good to the majority of people that doesn't know it." Irish had nearly vanished from his part of Mayo by the time he was born; most people had come to regard it as the speech of the backward and the uneducated, and that's the view Anthony, who considers himself an educated man, takes of it today.

He reserves for the tramp and the "travelin' beggar-man" the sort of high esteem that in other quarters is often lavished upon native Irish speakers. These men — Anthony calls them "the Lord's bards" — he met on the roads during his own traveling. He'd often (he says) recite one of his poems in exchange for a song he hadn't heard before, defying them to come up with a song he *hadn't* heard.

"Many of those men were high-strung persons, real aristocrats, and some were even educated, often in schools. You could tell from talking to them that they weren't the ordinary type of man at all. No, not at all ordinary."

Perhaps to some extent, these "bards" are Anthony's conscious models — the "furze" rising sharp within him. "If you want to talk of freedom," he observes, "those men had it. They didn't have to answer to anyone. Whether to go to Donegal town or to Enniskillen, the choice was in their own minds. That's why I call them 'the Lord's bards.' They had no master but the Lord."

The tramp, for him, is the apotheosis of all the old Irish traditions, a past master of the bright saying, a man with "every good crack and story that ever came about."

"One of those fellows I had met during my own travels came in on me back in Ballycastle about half a year ago, to stay the night, and he coughin'. 'A terrible cough, man,' I says to him. 'Yeah, 'twas cold in that barn last night.' 'You slept in a barn last night and it snowin' and hailin', Christmas time?' 'Yeah, yeah,' this was his speech, you know [Anthony speaks through his nose to imitate it], 'I'm Michael Walsh, Belmullet, County Mayo, yeah, I slept in a barn last night, 'twas cold.' 'My god, you'll get pneumonia, man, and die.' 'No, no, I couldn't die — I have never lived.'

"Fantastic wit he had — he had never lived, so how was he going to die?

"There was another fellow, a little raggedy man named O'Brien I met outside Claremorris sitting at the foot of a hill. He was closing his boot, and he had but one eye. 'Everybody must bear his cross,' he said, 'but 'tis strange, I can see more with my one eye than you can see with your two.' I heard one-eyed people say that before, and I never believed them before, so I says, 'Ah no, that's impossible for you to say.' 'All right,' he said, 'but will you bet it?' ' I will,' I says. He put two shillings down, and I put two shillings against it, and he beat me. He explained the case to me. 'I see your two eyes,' he said, 'but if you were looking at me, you can't see but one!'

"If you were talking with them till tomorrow, they could beat you. That was their lives, you see, between that and studying nature. And those men, I'm not coddin' you a bit, they were the purest gentlemen in the whole entire country! You wouldn't get a man with twenty servants and a landlord's big estate to touch them, for manners. They wouldn't harm a fly nor a flower. 'Twasn't a gentlemanly thing to lift my two shillings off me like that? Well, I ask you truthfully now, which is more gentlemanly, to lose two shillings to a beggar man, or to have the government take the lot of your money off you with taxes and high costs?"

Anthony jumps from here to a harsh indictment of the present government. Why, he asks, don't they raise subsidies for struggling bards like himself? Instead, all they seem able to raise is the price of a pint until no one can afford it. He spits out the car window to show his contempt, and the wind blows it back on him. He is not accustomed to riding in motorcars.

To decompose is to live too . . .
— Samuel Beckett, *Molloy*

When we reach his bungalow in Ballycastle, Anthony invites me in to share the simple comforts of his hearth, but advises me in advance that they really are simple, "because I have no chairs inside." In fact, I soon discover that there are no furnishings of any kind inside, only a lone mattress soiled to a rich golden-brown, the product of years of not washing. An odor of almost medieval rankness clogs the air, and the only light ("Long ago," says Anthony, "my electricity was taken away from me for non-payment of it") is that which the sun manages to scud in. It is the sort of home that only a person dedicated to his own home-lessness could love; the four walls are just an illusion, concealing just more Mayo bogland, which also surrounds them.

If Anthony is not proud of this domestic setting, neither is he ashamed of it. "A man could live in a dung pit and love it, I believe. In fact, I even knowed a man that lived in a public lavatory in Castlebar once. Would lock himself in a stall at night, pull his feet up when the guard came in to close it up."

"And a man could live in a barrel and love it, there's no doubt about that." He finds a half-empty bottle of Guinness on the floor, and hoists it to his mouth, and then in an effusion of scrappy phrases and asides, he goes on to describe his own past tenure in a barrel, "a grand ol' barrel I put up right near here." He had just returned to Ballycastle from his five years of musi-cal wandering, and what should he discover but that the roof of his ancestral cabin, the home of his father and his grandfather, had caved in from neglect? That was all right; he just began to live in this fishmonger's barrel he "put up" on his property, behind the original house. At least it provided him with a roof over his head. As for the other attractions of home, they could be obtained at the local pub.

(In the long run, he indicates, what difference will it make where he slept during that time? "There's no sleep in any of us, that won't be sleep when we come to God." His religiosity increases the more drink he's taken.)

He continued his residence in this barrel for the better part of a year. The end came suddenly. He never was able to brave the regimentation of turf cutting, and after sacrificing all the timber from his fallen house, he needed something else to burn, particularly with the advent of winter. So, he began raiding his neighbors' store of firewood, and also was not beneath taking the odd handle from a spade, for it made excellent seasoned kindling. Anthony speculates that one of his victims didn't take kindly to this last practice of his; late one night, he returned from the pub to discover a pile of charred wood where his barrel had been. Somebody had burned the barrel down. "I spent the next two days with a bottle of methylated spirits," he says, "I was that far gone with the sadness."

Anyway, the County Council took pity on him, and built him the bungalow where he now lives, and they supplied him with such furnishings as a respectable burgher might require. But within a week (and he refers to this with just a twinge of regret), he had sold everything but his mattress for "case after case of good Irish whiskey," which it took even him several months to drink. In that way, he transcended the sudden burden of middle-classness.

I gaze around the interior of the bungalow now, nearly twenty years after these events just described, and what the place seems to resemble most is — a cavernous barrel. Anthony has slowly staged a return to the days of his former glory, crawling back into his barrel as nearly as circumstance will allow. He has purified his living conditions of all nonessentials. Of the essentials, however, I am told to be very careful: Anthony says he never removes his boots anymore, for fear of stepping with his bare feet on the broken shards of bottles islanding the floor.

Custom usually dictates that a country person keep a tidy house, unless he's a bachelor and then he might be considered

somewhat disreputable (too "delicate") if his house is tidy.
Anthony's neighbors consider him disreputable anyway. They
give his bungalow a wide berth; their general attitude is a little
like that of the old mariners who refused to navigate the unknown regions that their maps labeled with "Here Be Mon-
sters."

"He's like a hippie or some suchlike person, he's so filthy."

"He's the worst man for booze I've ever met with."

"He let the house of his family fall in ruins without a bother
about it. Was that nice?"

"He's made a madhouse of his head."

Neighborly complaints like these have brought a regional social worker to Anthony's door on more than one occasion, and
he has not exactly warmed to this show of humane interest
toward his predicament.

"This chap from Ballina, he had been here before and each
time, 'twas a bit messy in the house. Well, he was a man with a
starch collar and a clean new suit. He came here about a month
ago and told me I should submit to 'psychoanalysis,' and I asked
him, 'What for?' and he said, 'Because we need to get you back
to normal,' and I says, 'I am normal, I've always been like this,'
and he says, 'But you need to talk to a doctor about your problems.' Well, I says, 'I got no problems, only I'm a fond man of
the pint, and sure, there's nothing wrong with that.' He says,
'We'll pay for your sessions and you'll see, they'll make a happy
man of you,' and I says, 'I'm not an unhappy man and this
"psychoanalysis" business, I don't know now but it mightn't
make an uhappy man of me.' 'All this dirt and filth you're
living in,' he says, ' 'tisn't fit for man nor beast,' and I tells him,
'I'm taking it the way God gave it to me, dirt and all.' So he kept
goin' on with the analysis stuff, like, and then he tells me, 'That's
what's getting our race into trouble, your kind of thinking,' and
now he's made me angry, you see, fuckin' angry, a stupid thing
that was to say to anyone, so I told him, 'I'm not the fuckin'
race, I'm meself, and I don't want any of your fuckin' analysis
even if the whole race is doing it.' He says, 'You can't go on like

this,' and I says, 'I'll go on all right, the same as you, except you're going first,' and I threw him out, told him to go away and not come back if he's going to talk such rubbish, about getting analyzed, imagine it."

At moments like the one he's just described, when the madness of the outside world seems to creep to his very doorstep, Anthony wishes he still had his concertina, for playing it "would clear the air of that nonsense." But having left this keyless instrument "somewhere on the road to Killala, he usually honors the departure of Benevolent Officialdom with a new verse. Or if it's the summer, he might find a degree of solace in one of the "hippie wanderers from all parts" who pass through and detect in him possibly some archaic counterpart to themselves. They've even given him marijuana seeds, and though he's sowed them, the plants were eaten by some sheep; this has happened twice, and Anthony therefore concludes that "sheep must be very fond of the marijuana." Yet he fears that even these people, sympathetic as they've been to him, might be rather put off by his habits: "There was a young Danish hippie-man staying with me for about a week, and he wanted me to go to his country and go on the tele for to be some sort of performer, because whatever I said, I made him laugh. He was trying to teach me the Danish language, you see, for that purpose. A flaming smart lad, yes — but I think he must have been used to another way of living than what I'm doing here, and when he left, he told me I should see a 'vocational guidance counselor.'

"What is a 'vocational guidance counselor'?" Anthony asks me.

Others, including Mr. Graves, have suggested that he try his hand at a profession, even engage himself with a bit of farming, like his father did, but Anthony feels that this might very well conspire against the dignity of the heroic past that he imagines for himself, deflating it with mundane sweat-work. And being the guardian of the bardic tradition, he is accountable to his fellow countrymen as well. He mustn't sully his role in society.

In fits of sobriety, however, and only then when he's presented with the gift of a young puck-goat, he might make a *bodhrán* (a skin drum played by traditional musicians), which might bring him fifteen pounds. But he can't bring himself to make an industry out of it with the purchase of a herd of goats. Such long-term investments are obviously not his style. Even, the purchase of an individual animal poses a nearly metaphysical problem for him: it is commerce in its rudimentary stages, and he cowers at the thought of it seizing him.

The skin of a greyhound, Anthony claims, will make the best *bodhrán,* because it is so thin, and a few months ago, he made one from an old greyhound belonging to a neighbor who was going to send the dog out to stud. The ensuing row landed him in court, where he was let off with a small fine by promising not to steal another greyhound. His day in court was a traumatic experience for him; since then, he hasn't made a *bodhrán* from any species of animal.

Anthony has been on the dole so long, remark his neighbors, he can't even remember another method of acquiring money. He himself likes to perpetuate the story that he hasn't worked, except in the bardic sense, since the last war. "I am the idle rich," he observes facetiously, nodding toward the empty Guinness bottles on the floor. But his face becomes quite serious at the memory of his wartime working days.

"I worked very hard for very little. In 1943, I left the old hearth and went to work on the docks of Belfast. I worked ten and twelve hours a day building ships — like a good many of the Irish working there, it wasn't for the war effort I was working, it was just to send a little money back to my parents sitting by the old hearthside and too old themselves to do any work.

"Well, if I was to describe tyranny right now, give you the proper definition of it, I'd call it tyranny to be working in the docks of Belfast. I hated my bosses — they weren't Irish to me. Stupid men, very stupid they were. And stupid work, too. I was even thinking of joining the Irish Army at that time, thinking anything would be better than just being a servant boy — until I saw one of them fuckin' bayonets, and they told me that the bayonet was to stick a man, and to turn it when it was inside in his carcass, to kill him, no, I'd have none of that. 'Twasn't in my nature, under any circumstance, to stick a human being with a weapon. Couldn't ever do it. I'd choose the slavery of the ship-building industry over that, any day of the year.

"Down at those docks, that was when I first put to memory Tom Moore, because I had his book in my pocket every day when I went down.

"Down there, I composed a good many of my own verses, too. What else was there to do, then? I just thought them up while I was down there, and I never had the chance to write them down, I didn't. The docks wouldn't fit you out with a desk and a pad of paper, y'know, so I just kept them there in my head, like I always done. I believe myself that if you write them down, you lose them, straight away; they'd fall out of your pocket, or they'd get burned up, or some accident would happen to them, I don't know what. But the ol' brains won't lose them, no. There's this in it too: I never seen any use in writing them down, and I could write you a letter, if I wanted, as well as you could write me one.

"I've been through the whole map of Ireland, and funny to tell you, I met all kinds of men, and I liked the most of the men I met, but I couldn't make my own of a man in Belfast. I couldn't feel that I should like him, because there was something poisonous in him, that if you were any other man from any other place, he was agin ye. 'Twasn't a very nice place, either. A very flat city, down low. The home of the Titanic.

" 'Twas in 1948 I quit that terrible business and hit the road, doing fairs and races with music and recitations. I wanted to get out of Belfast so fast, I left behind a new suit of clothes and a grand melodion. I just started walking, walking on. Belfast, what's left of it now, you could pack it into your back pocket and away with it."

Good God, what a land of breeders, you see quadrupeds everywhere.

— Samuel Beckett, *Molloy*

The raven bleeds around the eyes during coition. Anthony Fergus is a bird of a somewhat similar feather, for his own eyes are bloodshot from the intensity of his own indulgences. Except that for him, there has been no coition, not once by his own count; he remains untainted by that form of commerce as well.

"The closest that ever I came to courtin' came when I was a lad of twenty-five years and living at home. I had a pony, and this pony got sick with me, frosty, after Christmas it was, and there was nothing in it, only the bones. He couldn't eat nothing, and I used to be trying to give him old bran and turnips, one thing and another, and a sack over him for covering at night.

"Well, this one night, I was lying in my bed under the window, and I heard a horse galloping outside, and I looked out, and here was a big mare, the grandest mare, I never looked at a nicer one and she all snow-white and blue spots, and up upon the saddle was a young girl with long yellow hair. I never seen the like of her, lovely. She beckoned to me to come on, get up behind her, and what did I do but get up the way I was and it winter. Away we went, terrible cold weather.

"The next thing was, I came awake from my sleep and there I was, in my skin, no shirt or nothing, and I was on the back of my old pony between two big old rocks, no sign of the girl or mare or nothing. And we went down the rocks and between the old furze and I seen we were on a hill I knew very well, Knockannamaurnach they calls it.

"We went down the road about a mile where an old man lived. 'Twas about seven in the morning, and the old man said, 'What's wrong with ye at all?' 'I'm after comin' down from the mountain,' says I. He gave me a bad raggedy coat and terrible raggedy trousers, only one leg in them, and away I go in my bare feet leading the pony down the road to my own house here.

" 'Oh where have you been off to?' says my father. I was ashamed to tell him about the girl, do you see. 'I must have walked in my sleep or something,' I says.

"You see, that pony was sick and couldn't go nowhere, and there were bushes and rocks in it you wouldn't do in a week, the three miles in a week up to the top of that hill."

Anthony recites this tale with pride. He is glad to be detached from the rank and file of common courters. It is as if other peoples' accounts of the courting experience were only so much fabrication.

In his younger days, he was handsome enough, in a craggy way, to attract women from beyond this evanescent horsey set. Once or twice, he was even mistaken for Spencer Tracy on holidays. After the film *Boys' Town* first came out, one American lady, visiting relatives near Ballycastle, addressed him as "Father" and inquired how the work was going back in Nebraska. Anthony replied that indeed it must be going well, for the fine weather would mean the lads were all out cutting turf. The joke was lost on him until the local priest, informed of Father Flanagan's recent arrival in his parish, descended on him and warned him against impersonating men of the cloth.

He was handsome enough, except for one deformity: north Mayo. "By the time I was a grown lad, all the girls had gone away." That succinct sentence tells nearly the whole story; the remainder of it comes from the fierce love of celibacy men often pursue in the West as an alternative to loving not even *that*. Where there's scarcely a marriageable women around for miles, of what use is it to belabor the issue with hope? Instead, a man can become a monument of eccentric freedom, unfettered by a woman's influence. After a time, his desires will have dissolved as perfectly as a wafer in the mouth.

Of the fifty houses within a two-mile radius of him, Anthony notes that half of them lodge aging bachelors, stuck to their paltry holdings. In the same vicinity, there isn't a single aging spinster.

"My brother Pat is living in Pittsburgh in America and he has eight children and I have none. I've often wondered why the Creator wanted such a complete imbalance as that."

Despite his wondering, his face grows tenebrous at the chance of some woman luring him to the altar. After all, he's the last of the bards. What business does he have marrying? "Poetry and females, you wouldn't want to mix them together." He could not have accomplished all that he has, he states, if he had allowed himself to take the matrimonial plunge. The very thought of it causes him to wince, and brings a curse to his lips: "Women, they're bad news." Then, from the place in his mind where he stores such things, he breaks into a description of the bizarre practice of "spanceling," which an elderly man told him was common in Mayo "right up to a hundred fifty years ago."

"Ugly women that wanted a husband would work the spancel as a charm. They used to take the skin off a carcass of a person that was just after being buried. A band of skin from the waist right around the back, that was the 'spancel.' Dig up a dead man or woman from the burying ground for that purpose, to get the spancel. Then this woman would creep in and wrap the spancel around the waist of her intended man whilst he was asleep in his bed. The poor fellow, he wouldn't have a chance. If he didn't wake up while she's doing the wrappin', he'd have to marry her before the end of the year. And if he did wake up, then it's all over and he'll die before the end of that year. So you see, 'twas a very poor bargain altogether for the man. Ugly women they'd be — bad news."

I ask him if he thinks the odd ugly woman might be at it still.

"Well, it died out altogether. About the time of the Famine, that's when it would have died out. I expect 'twould be the contagion on the corpses put a stop to it."

But he is not amused, or not much. Spanceling has such far-reaching implications, the concept of it alone comes close to sobering him. It would seem to be the human condition, in a nutshell. Anthony has offered this little anecdote like a cautionary tale. His serious countenance seems to suggest that he thinks the *spirit* of the spancel lingers on in women — but he has had too little contact with them to know for sure.

"I wouldn't let no woman do me with marriage," he states, and as though to make certain that no woman is now approaching his bungalow with that thought in mind, he glances out the window over the giant navel-holes of his bog. No one is coming. The barren vista affirms yet another claim he can make to being the last; a line, stretching back to the beginning of time, will end with him.

The sudden downpour of rain does not deter Anthony from his everlasting pursuit of the pint. He whips into a long black frieze coat (which makes him look a little like Dracula), and we begin to negotiate the windy, well-nigh longitudinal rain for the mile-long trek to the nearest pub. Despite the wet, Anthony says that he prefers to walk this distance because walking may bring back the life to his injured foot.

At the bar are two youth hostelers instantly identifiable as Canadians by the abundance of maple leafs emblazoned on their rucksacks, jackets, and jeans. In the past, Anthony has found that Canadians are a good "touch" for marijuana. He walks up to one of them, shakes the fellow's hand vigorously,

and inquires, "Have you brought any of the green grass of home with you?" The fellow shakes his head; he doesn't quite understand. Anthony has to explicate the metaphor for him, which he does in a booming voice. No, neither of them carries that sort of thing. Then the boy's companion whispers something to him, and the two of them, indicating that they'd like to sit down, move to the opposite side of the room.

It is the odor of urine from Anthony that has done it; the original tanning properties from his coat (the wool for frieze is cured in urine for a year) have been released by the rain, and the smell has formed a nimbus around him for several feet. The other patrons of the bar are beginning to move away too, but that doesn't appear to bother Anthony, who is well used to their distance. He takes a long draft from his stout and looks at the bottle with the sort of intimate stare other men sometimes reserve for their women. Then suddenly he closes his eyes and recites what turns out to be his most recent composition, "The Football Match of the Fairies," machine-gunning the words in a manner that parodies radio sports announcers. It dramatizes a game of Gaelic football between a north Mayo team and a team made up exclusively of pookas, goblins, leprechauns, and assorted sprites. The mythical creatures win by one point; a Pyrrhic victory for the oral tradition.

We Are All Islands

Connaught is beginning to accumulate wealth again — people.
— "Connaught: Special Report," the *Irish Times*, July 29, 1975

The remaining five bachelors — all over seventy years of age —
who live on Owey Island, are ready to quit. They hope to find
new homes on the mainland before the winter sets in. Owey
had a population of close to 200 in the early twenties, but over
the years the young folk who emigrated were reluctant to
come back.
— The *Irish Press*, December, 1974

He sinks who carries the huge stones;
these stones I carried as long as I could
these stones I loved as long as I could
these stones, my destiny.
— George Seféris, "Gymnopaedia"

THE ISLAND OF Inishbofin is an interim of sea and mottled fields
six miles from the nearest peninsular arm of Connemara. People
come to it to gaze elsewhere, back at the cloud-dappled hills or
back at the sea, with its islets of porphyry.

Unlike the Synge-sung Arans, Inishbofin has not been a fortunate isle in story and song. No one has felt the compulsion to
squeeze romance or felicity from its wind-shorn heather. Perhaps, though desolate, it is not desolate enough ("My own

farmland here is so fertile," says one islander, "you could eat it with a spoon."). The newspapers sometimes confuse it with the other Inishbofin lying off the coast of Donegal, when provisions need to be helicoptered to either of them during the rough months of the winter. At one time, the British confused it with a lacuna where an island might have been; in the King's Books for 1810, the island's valuation was only ten shillings sterling, which would have just been enough to buy a pint of porter for one-tenth of the island's population (none of whom was later tempted to become Barry Fitzgerald, the Duke of Leinster, Brendan Behan, or a scion of the Guinness family).

Where the founding myths of other localities treat of birth, vitality, and general hopefulness, the legend of Inishbofin's beginnings has to do with death and petrifaction. Long years ago (so the story goes), the island was enchanted, uninhabited, and veiled by a thick mist. It might have been part mist itself, so phantasmal was its day-to-day existence. Finally, two fishermen lost at sea managed to navigate through the mist. Their boat crunched against the shingle of the north beach, and they landed, then lit a fire, which broke the island's spell. The mist lifted, and they saw an old witch driving a white cow toward them. The sight of the cow gave them a powerful thirst; despite the witch's protests, they began to milk it, but hardly had they grasped the cow's teats when the lot of them, including the cow, were turned to stone. The unnamed island was subsequently called "The Isle of the White Cow," Inish-bofin. The moral of the story is clear: beware the proximate tit in time of need, and hoard your precious fluids so you might live to see tomorrow.

As stone, these progenitors of the island are said to live on, but — where? Which stones? Inishbofin is littered with stones, they're the bones sticking through its skin, the sentries surrounding it: four headlands of ancient metamorphosed rock, schists and gneisses; outcroppings and islets, the names of which are miniature dramas in themselves, like Mweemringagweera, Daloughty, Loughanbeg, Mweelaundhru, Carrickmahoga, Mweelaundtrua, Mweeldyon, Carricknamweel; stone field-walls with phantom gates, built of stone; stones concealed under heather tufts; a rock in the harbor where Cromwell tied the Bishop of Clonfert, letting the incoming tide drown him; "The Stags," where two American students drowned recently; a pointed spire of a rock known locally as "The Monk's Penis"; two "famous" corn querns; and boulders peering out of the roads. How many of them are petrified people from the past? It is doubtful that the distinction between the rocks that are people and the rocks that are not will ever be made again on the island. In the cold north of Europe, life was thought to originate from the divine cow Audunla's licking of frozen stones, but on Bofin the divine cow is herself stone.

In its beginning is Bofin's end. The present time, too, is hag-ridden. "Bofin is a nice place to live if you have a nice small farm," says Patrick Lavelle, the island's oldest inhabitant, "but there isn't much people now at all. The great majority of the houses are closed. I'm here on my own, and half the houses are the same way. Soon there'll be no one left." "There's nothing, absolutely nothing for myself on this island," says a sixteen-year-old girl. "In Clifden [the nearest village on the mainland], at least there's a cinema, and there's a dance hall, too." Would she want to spend the rest of her days in Clifden, then? At this, she laughs. A joke. She is no heathen, can't you see?

What to do with this decrepitude? The loss of the young is preceding the loss of the old, and no one knows what to do about it. Two abodes exhibiting little sign of anxiety are the island's two pubs, located in its two small hotels. The older men go mostly to the one near the quay, it being fusty enough to suit their requirements; they dump the ashes and dottle from their pipes on the floor, to guarantee that this fustiness remains. Things are reciprocal here; just as each man of a group "stands a round" (despite the Irish government's current campaign against "rounds" and the wearing of badges which say "No Rounds, Please"), he will take his turn, whenever it comes, at the round of conversation. To depart the premises before the end of the last round would be thought vulgar. After all, this is a "public house," a place where everyone is cast into the implicit role of guest. The somewhat frowsy atmosphere makes sociability and certain confidences possible.

Scraps of conversation taken from an evening here:

"The grass for the sheep is so short this winter, the hair on your balls is longer."

"I was hauling freight into Houston, Texas, and you know who one of my mates was? The grandson of John Mitchel [the nineteenth century Irish patriot]. — "That's nothing. I went out with the great-great-grand-niece of Robert Emmet, in Blackburn, Lancashire."

" 'Tis a lie, there was no such thing as a moon flight. The sky was still as high as when we're looking at it now. They didn't get near it." — "But the pope received those men who went to the moon." — "The pope received them all right, but the pope should have gone with them to see for hisself."

"I went out to free Ireland and I a foolish young lad. I joined the I.R.A. during the troubled times, and I never got nothing out of it, only my hand was hurt and my knee was hurt."

"You must realize that an inch is a good deal on this island."

"Too much education is like too much food on the table. You feels sick afterwards."

"Pat McCann's gone to Australia to look after their sheep there." — "Sure, he can do that just as well right here on Bofin."

"I can't see them going on about President Childers now. When you're dead, you are like a cow — you're dead, and no more about it."

Some of these men refer to the presence in the other pub of "The Monster." Connoisseurs of the grotesque, they feel, assemble there to see it. "The monster" is a television, and possibly the modern reincarnation of the ancient mistress of the island, the old witch of its legend. Medusa-like, this creature also turns her victims into stone, stone-still and stone-quiet (" 'Tis like death," says Michael Joyce, an old fisherman. "One drink on the counter the whole time, and no man talking or making a bit of fun or anything.") Her visions of sugar plums dance seductively in their eyes, and it's the strong man who can refuse her offer of a liaison with *Born Free, Lost in Space, Dad's Army, The Wodehouse Playhouse, Superspy,* and *The Riordans.* There's hardly a defense against such rough magic, not on this small and vulnerable island. One is taught the absurdity of hobnail boots and chemical "loos," and of islands, when the rest of the world lives in the sparkle of its living rooms. Somehow, one must have begun life a mere gray clod in his mother's womb to end up in this gray donkey-world. Is it true Liverpudlians have more fun?

"The monster" courts mostly the younger people, who embrace her in order to accumulate the lore they will need later in life, elsewhere. Emigration begins "inside," as the Bofin man calls his island; it continues "outside," which is everywhere else. Departing the island is such a time-hallowed tradition that those who stay behind often seem guilty of deviant behavior. But now, observes Michael Joyce, "there's young people going away who are leaving it because of the entertainment — they won't find a job here or anywhere else, so they're only just going where the fun is now. They're going because they hate the old place. I don't see how a person can hate a place he was born on — even if you were born on top of a rock."

Back in west Kerry, perhaps just at this moment as Michael Joyce is pondering rock births, Tomás Walsh may be sitting down in front of his television to watch *Pillow Talk,* a favorite film in the West. Or he might be absorbed in a rerun of *Kojak* which by now he remembers as well as any single one of his stories. Yet it little matters that these alien images may be claiming his attention now. Tomás has long since accumulated *his* lore, his stories and *pishrogues* — for what they're worth. They were a part of his self-containment. Such things, in his day, could sometimes enchant islands, even islands on the mainland. But, as the late film mogul Sam Goldwyn was wont to say, "We have all passed a lot of water since then."

"We are getting more isolated now. No, I don't mean more isolated, I mean the opposite," says Michael Jack Burke, who knows Bofin the way Casals would have known his cello. "We

are all losing our identities, all to some terrible idea of inter-
nationalism. The canned American television is driving us to
think like — not to think at all. And we have joined the Rich
Man's Club, the E.E.C., but we are still poor creatures. It took
many years and trouble to drive out the Danes originally, and
the E.E.C. — why, it's the Danes all over again! 'Increase and
expand,' that is the motto of today, but my own feeling is, the
large wildcat grandiose schemes should be broken down into
smaller schemes, and we should be thinking smaller and smaller
instead of larger and larger. We are all islands — Bofin, Ireland
— and each island (to turn around John Donne) stands alone."

No man knows more about the elusive, nearly indetectable
currents that flow beneath the surface of this half desolate, half
arable island than Michael Jack. No man on Bofin is more an
island, standing alone, than himself. His human fortress is will-
fully difficult of access — like his own house, which lies at the
end of a trough-like path usually flooded, the next-to-the-farthest
dwelling from the modest bustle of the harbor area. Close by,
closer than this harbor, is Inishshark, an island devoid of people
since 1962, resting there on the sea, Michael Jack says, "to remind me of my mortality." He says that Inishshark died because
its bad harbor forced it to become dependent upon Bofin for its
staple goods, and since Bofin by then had become mostly dependent upon the mainland for *its* goods, "that put poor Shark
two removes from the source of everything. Their fishermen had
to row over to us for *our* Norwegian fish fingers."

He utters this last insight with an exaggerated stress on the
sibilants. Disgusting it is, to purchase frozen Norwegian fish
fingers in a place which is itself "the home of the fish." Michael
Jack believes in the eternal verity of isolationism, buttressed by
subsistence fishing and farming. He even practices it in his personal dealings. *Noli me tangere* is his program for every make of
island, including the confines made by his own flesh.

One of his fellow islandmen describes Michael Jack as "per-
manently pissed." Even if it is usually expressed with greater

propriety, he does have that reputation on the island. Very likely this comes from his fondness for remarks like "People are a curse on this earth," which he offers as public proclamations. Yet, by this, he does not mean to wound. It is a commonplace, like the bad weather. "People are a curse" — for Michael Jack, at least that's something. "I've often thought that the reason we once had so many wonderful personalities on this island resulted from venom and hostility. Everyone hated everyone else so much, they had to be different in order to survive. They took themselves in their own hands, you might say, and proceeded to make themselves different, just as you'd get up and build a new house or byre out of the stone of the old one. There wouldn't be a man on the island who wouldn't have ten, twenty, and thirty other men against him. Yes, that is true. Too much sameness spoils the brew, they say, and these people, all they wanted to be was — themselves. But of course they'd still help each other in their work, help a man thatch his haystack during harvest time." Michael Jack intimates that this tradition is integral to his own nature; he cultivates himself, and pursues what he calls "my inviolable core of solitude." A "literary" phrase, but then Michael Jack is a "literary" man.

Would he not like to be deposited on Inishshark, to live out his days away from the plague of his fellow man? He shakes his head. No, that would never do, for he does like to *observe* people — from the settled distance of his own choosing, inside himself. In a way, he is like a novelist, collecting tics and foibles for their fictional value. But his "novel" has never gone farther than his own talk. Is he — the island storyteller, then? A few of the islanders think that's what he might have been, if instead, he hadn't grown this spiny carapace. The island is proud of Michael Jack, of his intellect and his wide reading ("Michael Jack has read the world over," they say). But its relation to him has never been that of a submissive, wondrous audience. All too often he has scared away his potential "audience" through his gruffness, or he has talked of the sex novels of D. H. Lawrence, which amounts to the same thing.

Michael Jack's detachment from his people corresponds to the distance they themselves have traveled from the time such a social role might have been his; storytelling, during Michael Jack's fifty-six years on the island, has not been a possibility. Where have all the old stories gone? "Into books," Michael Jack comments. By a curious trick of time, he is like Seán Murphy fifty or a hundred years later, steeped in books and altogether more recent stories. The new stories have a value of their own, and to illustrate this, he turns on his wireless just in time for a BBC Special Program and Malcolm Muggeridge, who is poised to explicate some of his own arcanery. "I like Muggeridge. I like him because he believes 'Backward, Christian Soldiers.' "

Ho, talk save us.

— James Joyce, *Finnegans Wake*

"The only reason I talk to anyone anymore is to keep myself warm," says Michael Jack. But when he *is* moved to talk, often he'll advance into a monologue as self-contained as an aria, and then, possibly, one comes near to listening to an island story-teller, even if this monologue is only a description of how he removes cysts from a sheep.

It might even be a peculiar variant of storytelling when a woman visitor to the island stops to watch him remove one of these cysts and he regales her with Robert Graves's "Down, Wanton, Down":

> Down, wanton, down! Have you no shame
> That at the whisper of Love's name,
> Or Beauty's, presto! up you raise
> Your angry head and stand at gaze?

"None of them ever seems to understand what the 'wanton' is. When you realize that they've spent their formative years going to mass, it isn't surprising. I'm only surprised that they don't answer 'The Sacred Heart' when you ask them their name."

Another eccentric? Michael Jack has progressed beyond Anthony Fergus because, of course, he has heard of Homer. The trouble is, there is no one with whom he can talk of Homer. The story has it that he once met a professor from Dublin on the road near his house, and the conversation turned to Gogol, Tolstoy, and Dostoevski. When the man finally bid him goodbye, Michael Jack is supposed to have grabbed him by the lapels, and said, "I've waited thirty years for this, and I'm not going to let you get away so easily now." But being already late for the mailboat, the professor could only apologize and dash away. The brevity of these encounters does not bother Michael Jack. He is used to brief encounters. He just returns to his fields, and addresses himself to the problem of sheep cysts, which is another kind of encounter, one that is less brief.

Books have become Michael Jack's shanachies. But, like Anthony Fergus, he still remembers whatever reaches him in the shape of poetry. Once a poem has been engraved into his mind, there's no forgetting it, from one of Dylan Thomas's more gnomic offerings to Rudyard Kipling's "If," everything, regardless of its quality. Michael Jack does not find anything extraordinary in this facility. "Poetry is stuck inside you. It will hold in you." Visitors to the island have experienced this retentiveness in reverse, for poetry will not hold in him. Once they've brought him to the stage of recitation — for them, he's a lark, a pleasantly meaningless grotesquerie, and to him, all visitors are the same, "a bloody pestilence" — he won't break off until he's finished, even if that means the whole of Gray's "Elegy in a Country Churchyard," rendered with an involvement that would almost indicate that the elegy concerns Inishbofin and its own buried lives, this graveyard island of weathered homes slanting from its hillsides. Once, Michael Jack pursued an Englishman, who had fled his "Ancient Mariner," down the entire length of the island, shouting the lines of the poem at him as he went.

It may be that this sort of thing represents the storyteller in him, too. And perhaps these one-man shows, like the monologues, function like storytelling sessions in his mind. They are served up with just the right panache to suggest a vastly older form of entertainment. But whatever else they are, they are also fugitive rituals, even directed toward fugitives and entailing pursuit.

One part of Michael Jack's mind embraces the larger world; another part is spliced to the inveterate rhythms of Inishbofin, the turf cutting and sheep dipping, and the western wind that makes a rag of the island in the winter. Michael Jack knows that he has been subject to the influence of his reading, that neither Dylan Thomas nor Frantz Fanon could remain planted in one place, but strange to say, seldom does his sense of "the outside" blur what he takes to be the dignity of labor in his own fields. He also knows that it is a cliché, indeed a literary cliché, to be gratified by such plain labor, and still, he is.

Too many successive generations of his own family have endured the island for him to entertain the idea of leaving it. "I wouldn't ever leave, not even if the whole American Army brought tanks and machine guns to drive me off." He is *of* the island, or his spirit is. Nonetheless, when he has just finished discussing (for example) Robert Falcon Scott's Antarctic journals and his enthusiasm for them, it still comes as an astonishment to hear him shift to those island "characters" so dear to the memory of his boyhood, he calls their houses "the only *authentic* churches I went into when I was growing up here." Suddenly, one remembers: he's still only a small farmer, pinioned to a small island, obliged to spend his life among these people the best of whom Captain Scott might have found pleasantly meaningless eccentrics. The feeling of this change in Michael Jack is rather like watching Dr. Jekyll transform himself abruptly into a Mr. Hyde able and determined to elucidate his own view of things. Traces of the island brogue, a rapid sounding of words designed to be heard above the wind, begin to surface in his own more "educated" speech.

"There was one man, Mike Daly, and he had as grand an imagination as you'd find in any book. I believe he had even perfected a method for blowing his nose in the palm of his hand and ridding himself of the results in one quick movement, so that the stuff would literally not touch his hand.

" 'Twas just after a man who had the reputation of a notorious rake had died on this island — a man merry with girls and even older women — that Mike performed his masterpiece. His *magnum opus*. They were waking this rake in his own house, and the corpse was laid out in its coffin on four chairs. Then Mike came in to the house, whistling. He would always be telling me he had great courage, that he was never afraid of a dead person. So he walked right up to the corpse, and he reached into his pocket, and he pulled out a French letter and placed it right over the penis of the dead man. ' 'Twouldn't do,' he said, 'him putting worms and vermins in the family way!'

"You know, this is folklore. Mike had almost certainly invented a new breed of wake game. They have all that stuff in the Irish Folklore Archives up in Dublin, and it's all run through the Puritan mill. No French letter ever got into the Irish Folklore Archives, I'll bet. It wouldn't be let in if it was concealed in a prayer book. And still, there was more folklore in it, what Mike did, than in all the Saint Brigid's crosses in Ireland, and all the cures for warts and shingles.

"Old Con Schofield was another man, and I think for once, a man was given his proper name. Because that's what he was — an "old con." I suppose you might call him a storyteller. He'd make up the wildest stories on the spot, impromptu, all at once. You'd be out cutting the turf, and he'd be there too. And as soon as he'd see you, he'd stop with his work, and walk over, and — out it came! I remember once that he told me — out in the bog,

as was his custom — how he fought with Napoleon at the Battle
of Austerlitz and how he had been decorated by Napoleon for
his bravery there. To prove this, he reached into his pocket for
the medal, and he looked worried when his hand came up with
nothing. 'Well, I must have dropped it t'other day over at Lyon
Island collectin' winkles,' he said. I told him that he was codding me. 'Damn it, man,' I said. 'You're too young to have
fought with Napoleon,' which was probably the compliment he
wanted from me all along. This was about 1937, and if he had
been at Austerlitz, he'd need to be at least a hundred and fifty
years of age, instead of only eighty. The truth meant no more to
him than fiction. Facts were only servant girls. You'd call him
up, and then he'd start all over again telling you about the part
he played during the Troubles smuggling German guns in from
Bofin to the I.R.A. He'd talk you completely dead, and he hadn't
a tooth in his mouth, just mashing his gums together there like a
sow pig's ass.

"I'll tell you, it was all in the way they said it. I think it comes
from the years of English domination, when the way they talked
kept them alive. Kept their culture alive. You see, they daren't
speak of Ireland then at all. They'd call her a maiden, and when
they spoke of her or sang of her, the invaders sat with them, but
they didn't know who they were singing about. There wouldn't
be a woman in sight, sometimes not until you got into the next
county. But she was Ireland all along. They said they loved her
and they wanted her to be free. It wouldn't do for the poet to
say in his songs, 'We're going to free Ireland and we're going to
be rebels.' He'd be up at the next wall and shot!

"Now with ourselves, it was the very same thing with regard
to that kind of symbolic talk. For example, there was more talk
about sex, more cracks about sex, on this island when I was a
lad than there is today, with the so-called free sex and free love.
There wouldn't be the usual four-letter words, of course, and
that was partly because we'd think they were uncivilized, partly
because we were afraid the local priest might be listening —

and there'd be a penance to do. So, we used to have words invented for those words. I remember Mike Daly coming back from Manchester, England, after his first year there, and I remember his description of his first female conquest. He said she was loose and easy, and of course, this surprised us, in a woman. Then he said she was so easy, ' 'twasn't two ticks when I had her rid of her dress and down to her carrigeen moss.' He was talking of her quim, and he turned to us and said, all wide-eyed, 'Well, lads, 'twas a city in itself!'

"All that has changed, changed utterly, as our friend Yeats would say."

One small, archaic object in Michael Jack's possession has survived this change reasonably intact — the literal tongue of Paddy John Halloran, a man remembered by the island as the last of its traditional storytellers. This tongue is Michael Jack's inheritance from his father, who clipped it from the dead man's mouth during his wake. For an odd shibboleth, once practiced occasionally on some of the more remote western islands, allowed that a storyteller's tongue, as though a rich store of words in itself, might be passed from the deceased to his living successor . . . and then either chewed or eaten whole, for its verbal nutrients. "My father took that tongue only for amusement's sake, and I don't think he ever chewed on it. I never heard a single story escape from his mouth," says Michael Jack.

By the time the tongue had reached him, "a different set of values was in the air," and the custom of ingesting tongues was considered unhygienic, if not downright pagan. This tongue, anyway, is too valuable to be swallowed. Michael Jack keeps it in an empty tin of Three Nuns' tobacco, where it rests cheek-by-jowl with the condiments, and from time to time, he brings it out for visitors to gaze upon and wonder. The vaccum-tight tin holds it back from a rapid decay, but this once-staunch midwife for the stories of a generation still resembles a piece of desiccated tripe left in the Sahara for years, so gnarled and hard and blackened has it become. "A lovely little thing," says Michael

Jack of his prize possession. "I wouldn't part with it for the new one million pound Univac computer they've just given to the Connemara Gaeltacht." Clearly, this tongue is his version of the Legion of Honor.

"A complicated man," says one of his neighbors of Michael Jack, echoing the sentiment of the island, which finds it difficult to "place" him. Western people do not like to think of themselves as complicated. So, is Michael Jack one of them or not? His "learning" is a wonderful thing, surely, but then again, he thinks that tourists to the island are "a bloody pestilence," humanly and economically, and he refuses to play up to them in the summer. Then there is the matter of mass, which Michael Jack doesn't attend ("The most solemn affairs are always the ones that are the most ridiculous. It's the right fool who can't laugh at the idea of high mass"). This means that he has is-landed himself away from the lone all-Bofin social event of the week; it also means that his mind must remain a greater mystery to the other islanders than it would be if on public display before the mysteries of the mass. What else could he be doing on Sunday mornings? "I'm either listening to the BBC on my wireless, or out on the hill, if it's lambing time, helping my ewes." Michael Jack says that he prefers the company of dogs and sheep to that of people. The island retaliates by calling him an "atheist."

Ten miles north of Bofin, the philosopher Ludwig Wittgenstein, another solitary, spent a winter near the little Connemara village of Renvyle. Though it was in 1947, local people still remember Wittgenstein for the austerity of his habits and the wild seabirds he tamed by talking continually to them in German. It is rumored that he'd stand so long in concentration among the rocks, seagulls would begin to settle on him. During this time, he subsisted mostly on corn flakes. "A simple man," says a Renvyle farmer who knew Wittgenstein. "A simple and plain man."

"Last summer, the tourists gave off the worst odor we've had on this island since an old billy goat was brought here some years ago."

Michael Jack's hostility to tourists has resulted in his disbarment from the Bofin pub nearest him, the one containing "the monster." One evening late last summer, he could stand it no longer; he assaulted a holiday-making businessman from Cork city. "This well-groomed individual was going on and on about turning the island into a luxury tourist resort, an ocean-going Killarney, like, with beach houses, sauna baths, private clubs, the whole damn lot. I asked him how he would compensate the people of the island for their loss of liberty. He said 'Bugger your liberty' or something like that, and I said that's what you'll be doing if you succeed in your venture. He became abusive — he had a few pints on him — and I landed a punch on him that the late John L. Sullivan would have been proud of. You see, I'm not Bord Failte's best ambassador in this country." But he says this action has chastened him somewhat; he no longer hits tourists. Instead, he has conditioned his dogs to do his bidding; he need only utter the word "tourist," and his three dogs, snapping and barking, dash out the door and onto the road to menace the unsuspecting passerby.

These people are mostly urbanites from Dublin and Cork,

and Michael Jack regards them as his inferiors: "They don't think for themselves the way we do inside in here. They change their wives the same way we'd buy and sell a hog." He rather resents their poking about *his* island in an orgy of leisure, "interrupting me to ask what it is I'm doing when it's plain to any damn fool I'm helping a cow that's just after calving."

Such people, he says, "don't like to see life in a place. They don't like an ague-marked face between them and a fine view of Bofin harbor. They don't like the smell of sweat to come between them and the wind, when they're not doing any sweating themselves. They like it all empty, open and empty, and I fear myself that they're going to get it before long. I see where Bord Failte is sinking fifty million pounds into a tourist development plan over the next five years. Damn it, man. That same money could be going to employment in the West. To keep people from leaving. Not into telegraphing the hundred thousand welcomes across the sea, to Siberia for all I know.

"Each year I see more young lads and girls leave the island, leave it forever, and each summer brings in more of the tourist class. The connection is so obvious I won't belabor it. Before long, it'll be all over.

"Once, there was a sense of joy to a small place. To say you were from that place. A sense of superiority, and none of this 'development' nonsense. The MacNeil, the clan leader of the island of Barra in the Hebrides, would go to the battlements of his castle after dinner, and he'd yell out, 'Hear! Hear! The MacNeil of Barra has just eaten! The other princes and kings of the earth may now dine on their dinners!' And to think, Barra is an island no bigger than Bofin. . . . I wonder if they're getting no more for a sheep there than they got in 1955. Sure, we get no more than that here.

"Tourists never made a marriage."

He is right, there. They never made a marriage except within their own "class," at holiday hotels. A Dublin girl wouldn't marry into a Bofin family today, "unless she had a death wish," Michael Jack says. "She might find our island a nice place to visit, but like the cliché, she would never want to live here. She'd feel she was better off in a Soviet labor camp. At least she'd think she was working for the future there." Likewise, he adds, the traditional proposal of marriage on the island would hardly lead a woman to think she had much of a future *there*. "The island lad doesn't ask a girl to marry him. He asks her, Wouldn't she like to be buried with his people?"

It is too late to fight this sort of death. Michael Jack has now given up on what he calls "my grandiose schemes" to lure women to the island. A few years ago, he put an advertisement in the *Connaught Tribune*, on behalf of the island's bachelors, divulging "the urgent need for wives of forty-five bachelors living on an island paradise." The only responses came from married couples, who requested further information about the "island paradise."

To stick a western island with the tag of "paradise" is a tacit admission of defeat. Michael Jack first made this admission long before his publication of the sexual imbalance on Inishbofin. He made it whenever he decided (if it was a decision with him) not to join with the women who lay over the sea, but to remain behind with his own lands, in a marriage performed without benefit of a priest. From that, all else flowed — or did not flow.

It is too late, and Michael Jack has gone beyond mere human caring. What remains is just a joke: the wit inherent in last things, his own. "The small farmer of this island spills his seed on the ground, when he should be sowing it." "The men of Bofin can 'hold their own' against the world." He is fond of double entendres like these. And he takes a certain pleasure in declaring his celibacy for all to hear ("I'm as celibate as an old billiard ball"), saying that "everything I know about sex, I've learned from the breeding of livestock."

He is so remote from sex, he can treat it in this fashion, as though it were a new and dubious gadget, a farrago of absurd parts; he can only marvel in comic terms at such a weird invention. But then life itself is only a comedy of errors to him, sweeping him along, a small error, these fifty-six years with its snarled netting. "I didn't ask to be born. That means I am an error, doesn't it-"

Sometimes, Michael Jack likens himself to the sort of monk who would have thrived on Inishbofin in the early Middle Ages, after Saint Colman, coming from Lindisfarne in Northumberland, had established a religious settlement on the island. But this is a sex joke as well. For it wasn't Michael Jack's own choice, in the beginning, that drove him to adopt monastic habits; it was the island's choice. And though, monklike, he is hibernating for the duration, there is a hard rind around his heart much of the time.

Short-lived is a man away from his native place and his sheep.

— Old Irish proverb

There remain his animals: one donkey, three dogs, six cows, and forty sheep. They have become his many "mates." When he reflects on them, his eyes appear to sink deep in his brow as through a surfeit of sight. For most of his day, he must inhabit their experience; and now they've turned into the rocks that anchor him to his own experience. They are not a "curse" deranging the earth. Nor are they winsome Disney child-minds. Quite the contrary. Michael Jack says that he enjoys the companionship of his animals because of their complexity, because of the secret, subtle ways their lives unfold and finally enrich his. Indeed, he believes that their lives are forsworn to meditation, rather like his own, and he dares anyone to prove otherwise. "A person doesn't know animals who says that their minds are incapable of thought. The common idea is that all men think and that all animals have instinct. My own belief is, it's the other way around — animals have a better balance of reason and instinct than most men I've met."

These animals have made a bestiary of his mind.

Closest to him is his eldest dog Mike, who was named for Michael Jack's old friend Mike Daly. This spotted mongrel takes on something of the character of an eldest son — except that, should Michael Jack happen to die, his inheritance would probably be a bullet through the brain to prevent his savaging of sheep. Often, Michael Jack will speak to this dog of abstruse subjects, like Bertrand Russell's rejection of Christianity. And on these occasions, Mike is a truly captive audience; he only interrupts the quiet of his listening to emit a fart. Owing to a stomach malady, he trails farts wherever he goes, in the house and outside, endlessly. The pungent odor is of deteriorated body organs. There's no cure for it, Michael Jack says. "It's just age with him. He's only just farting out the dead inside him, so he can live on. You get used to the smell, and it becomes no worse than any other smell you'd happen to have around." Mike is always sidling up to Michael Jack, sniffing affectionately at him.

The youngest of his dogs is named Paddy John, after the old storyteller whose tongue Michael Jack owns. Like his namesake, Paddy John's tongue is forever wagging after visitors . . . but to ward them off with growls, barking, and other suggestions of violence. "If I saw a person kicking a child, I'd tell him to stop, and failing that, I'd pull the child away. But if I saw a person kicking Paddy John, I'd kill that person . . ." A splendid sheep dog, Paddy John "handles sheep with the same gentleness I'd use myself. He knows his trade like a master." By now, this dog has become Michael Jack's personal emissary to the world of sheep and men.

When I have such friends as these, Michael Jack implies, how could I ever be lonely? And how could it be called loneliness when I live in such proximity to all of nature — there is the sea, the mountains, the other western islands, "the whole works," he says, and "don't forget the sunset on Boughil and Cailleen. They turn the color of amethyst during a good sunset."

Boughil and Cailleen are two rocks on Inishshark visible from his fields. Once, the story goes, an island girl tempted a boy to sin, with the result that they were transformed into these rocks, Boughil the boy and Cailleen the girl. "Their souls are supposed to be eagles nesting in those rocks," says Michael Jack. "But I don't remember a time when there were ever eagles nesting there."

Envoi: The Vanishing

"You have only to press that button and the people of the house will hear a bell ringing within."
Cause for laughter from God! said I to myself, if I happened to be alone and to come to that door, it is the toe of my boot it would get . . .
— Maurice O'Sullivan, *Twenty Years A-Growing*

The island. A last effort. The islet. The shore facing the open sea is jagged with creeks. One could live there, perhaps happy, if life were a possible thing, but nobody lives there. The deep water comes washing into its heart, between high walls of rock. One day nothing will remain of it but two islands, separated by a wide gulf, narrow at first, then wider as the centuries slip by, two islands, two reefs. It is difficult to speak of man under such conditions."
— Samuel Beckett, *Malone Dies*

WINTER. A leaden Atlantic mist has abolished the mainland of Kerry, giving way only when the wind, the king of the oldest keening, slashes irregular holes in it. Then bits and pieces of land are visible, for the moment.

Across the velvety runs of rabbits, I walk to land's end, to where the three heather humps of An t-Oileán Mór, the Great Blasket, become churlish sea again. This island, which is five miles long and one mile wide, is the Ultima Thule of Europe, the westernmost point before "the next parish" of America, toward which, on maps, its narrow shape is a wizened, accusing finger.

At the very end, near the detritus of some beehive huts, I find a dead ewe, dying in birth, its carcass and the carcass of its new lamb picked almost clean. The remains are sprinkled with roasted coffee beans — maggot shells. Likely, the ravens gouged out the ewe's eyes as she was lambing, then killed her when she couldn't see to struggle. During the lambing season, the islanders used to stand watch over their sheep with shotguns, because it was then when they were vulnerable that the ravens would try to get them. Now, the remaining islanders graze the Blasket from the mainland.

This island has fulfilled the geographical destiny of "the West." It has become a landscape of death, and to walk on it today is to know the myriad shapes of death.

The skins of rabbits turned inside out, the toy bones floating on the stunted heather like a Tanguy painting. The husks of shags, fulmars, and puffins the tide delivers. In an old shed, a dead goat preserved in an attitude of writhing; outside, another goat, perhaps its mate, rotted to a skull and vertebrae. A seal washed up on the shingle strand in a wreath of seaweed, a face that is almost human.

Stone deaths, the plenitude of ruins. Beehive cells and the final, undistinguished rocks of a neolithic fort. The Martello tower, struck by lightning — a Stonehenge of brash. The houses at the butt end of the island, in a state of original sin, clustering together like survivors on the stern of a lifeboat. Thistle at nearly all the doorsteps. Under their open roofs, they share the same epitaph.

"In the end, we could only mount the crew of three curraghs, there were so few of us," says a former islander. "Then the last winter there, a boy died without priest or doctor, and that frightened us. When we saw there was no marriages and no young people growing up, we wanted to come to the mainland, but it wasn't from our hearts we wanted to come." On March 23,

1953 — the same day as the first Everest expedition established its base camp — this last dragglement of twenty-eight islanders was transferred to Dingle, on the mainland. A local legend has it that one dissenter escaped relocation by hiding near Ceann Dubh, at the far west of the island. Once, he was seen on the south cliff scaling its bird-fretted crannies in search of gulls' eggs; a few people have observed his face, a wilderness of hair, peering out at them from behind rocks. But he has never spoken.

There hadn't been a wedding dance on the Great Blasket since 1937.

The Blasket people call their departure from their island "the vanishing." They use that expression to refer to past time. An event has happened either before or after "the vanishing." In a sense, they are living beyond their own disappearance.

Twenty years after this vanishing, an American, Taylor Collings, purchased most of the island, buying it up plot by plot, field by field. Only three bachelor brothers, formerly of the island, refused to sell to him. "We still wanted to have access to our homeland," they said. Before long, Mr. Collings had published a flyer announcing the birth of "The Blasket Island Ranch, Situated on the Serene, Enchantingly Beautiful, Pollution-Free, Europe's Closest Inn to America." But death is inviolable, if pollution-free. Mr. Collings was not allowed to dump new houses on the island, owing to the fact that the County Council had proclaimed it a Restricted Development Area: a fine irony of words for a place whose people, even in the end, had no choice but to be impervious to development. So he had to content himself with rubble — or with renovation.

At the time of this writing, Mr. Collings has renovated three of the island dwellings. One of these houses belonged to the legendary storyteller of the Blasket, Peig Sayers, Peig Mhór — Big Peig. "The Dáil" her house was called, or "talking place," taking its name from the Irish parliament. Here Peig held her sessions: her nocturnal feasts of words, an endless pouring of stories, fables, and anecdotes. One of the former islanders remembers one of her shortest anecdotes: "Peig once told us about Aristotle's wife, who called for him to tell her the whole lot of his wisdom. He consented to this — if your woman would only sit naked on a cold stone to listen to him, which she did and soon after died of the exposure." Wisdom, in the Blasket, begins with knowing the sanest way to obtain it.

Another renovated house has been set up with the bar from *Ryan's Daughter*, a gift from the director, David Lean. Summers, this house offers cups of tea to day-trippers, who mightn't know that when crates of tea were first wrecked on the Blasket one hundred years ago, the substance was taken as a species of brown dye. But in the winter, there is nary a day-tripper, and westerly gales return the island to what it is, self-absorbed, bereft of people. These gales give the island a constant wailing, but they cannot give it the coherence of speech. For that reason, the difference between a Restricted Development Area and an Egregious Development Area is ever so slight: it can be measured in amounts of photographs and in the scenery for movies. In *Ryan's Daughter*, the Blasket loomed in the background in several scenes; some of the former islanders were even asked to play weathered villagers, which they had never been — until then.

This is a crag in the midst of the great sea, and again and again the blown surf drives right over it before the violence of the wind, so that you daren't put your head out any more than a rabbit that crouches in his burrow in Inishvickillaun [a neighboring island] when the rain and the salt spume are flying. . . .

You may understand from this that we are not to be put in comparison with the people of the great cities or of the soft and level lands. . . .

It was a good life in those days. Shilling came on shilling's heels; food was plentiful, and things were cheap. Drink was cheap, too. . . . That's all gone by now, and the high heart and the fun are passing from the world. Then we'd take the homeward way together easy and friendly after our revelry, like the children of one mother, none doing hurt or harm to his fellow.

. . . it was my wish that somewhere there should be a memorial of it all . . . for *our like will not be there again.*

— Extracts from the conclusion of *The Islandman,* Tomás Ó Crohàn's Blasket Island autobiography

Extracts from a conversation with Tomás Ó Crohan's son Seán, who left the Blasket in 1944 to live in the west Kerry village of Murreigh:

"My father Tomás was a good talker and a good fisherman, too. He used to have a bit of paper in his pocket, and a pencil, and anything at all that would happen during the day — let it be the braying of an ass — he'd describe it down on paper, right there. . . .

"We had nothing but fishing. Sheep, maybe. . . .

"The Blasket people were very healthy — like a trout. The eating was the cause of it. Plenty of fish and *bairneachs* [limp-

ets]. I saw an old man on the Blasket Islands, and he was one
year before one hundred, and he was just like a big barrel —
he wasn't tall, but he was a well-rounded man! . . .

"It was three miles beyond the limit, and they maintained
they shouldn't have to pay taxes because of it. They stoned any
bailiff who would set foot on their soil. In my father's time, they
also stoned a botanist, because they thought he was a bailiff. . . .

"A good pint, yes . . .

"The man who wouldn't sing and dance and tell stories and
look after the girls, he'd be half-cast out altogether. He'd be no
good. If he hadn't any of those things, they'd bolt the door on
him! They'd say he was half-gone. . . .

"The lads on the island, they were mad after the girls born on
the island, but the girls wouldn't take any notice of them —
they'd rather 'go to the moon.' They wanted to leave and meet
strange boys. And some parents didn't want a boy to go to a
certain girl's house. 'You may as well put your hand on the
moon,' they would say to him, 'It would be easier for you to put
your hand on the moon than to go to that woman's house.' They
had a hard time with a family themselves, and they didn't want
that business to start again. . . .

"I don't mind about any religion — my religion is from the
shining of the sun. The sun and the moon and the stars, all the
people on the island were going for them. . . .

"I know the island as well as I am here. I know that well that
never again will people live in the Blasket Islands. Even in my
own last days there, there was grass growing through our paths
and roads, for want of walking on them."

Seán met his own extinction beyond sight of the Blasket.
Ironically enough, it happened on the bland pavement at the
end of his life, not on the sea, which he had fished for fifty years,
resisting the most treacherous waters in the British Isles. On
December 8, 1975, in the dark of early evening, he was struck
by a lorry near his house and died of internal injuries and shock.
At seventy-seven, he still walked the two miles to the public
house in Ballydavid each evening; he was just beginning that

walk when he was hit. "I could never be myself here, would you believe it? I was too advanced when I came here," he had confided to me toward the end of our conversation.

I am trying to place the meaning of all this death against the calamity of contemporary Ulster and *its* deaths, and even as I write, here on the Great Blasket with an oyster catcher pip-pipping its warnings overhead, my portable wireless announces that a Catholic road-sweeper has been found with his throat cut in a Loyalist area of west Belfast. Minutes later, it reports that a Protestant has been shot dead, in a nearby house.

And so it goes on, measure for measure, the grotesque logic of reprisals, the falcon hastening farther from the falconer. "I thought it was only a lorry backfiring," reports a woman to the police: it was a few pounds of gelignite, put beneath a school bus. "Murderers . . ." says a prominent clergyman. But does he include in this category the eight-year-old who busies himself with the throwing of a Molotov cocktail at army vans? "Disgraceful . . ." says an English M.P. in parliament. He must think this violence extremely ill-mannered, like a faux pas at teatime. What is a small island off the coast of west Kerry to *that* disgrace?

The Republicans say that every act of violence no matter how small, even the mundane maimings, brings their Irish island closer to an authentic Republic.

"We had a Republic of our own," says Micheál Hurley, a former Blasket man who confesses he can't keep pace with the present troubles in the North, as they disclose themselves by means of his television. There are too many politicians screaming across frontiers, too many factions and splinter factions, and too many dead, their numbers shot out at him too quickly. The sea never took Blasket fishermen in such abundant numbers; and when it took them, it did so more realistically, not in framed, silvery images. Of course, he knows what he feels: horror. He muses on the instability of the situation, the truces, the destruction, and comes up with — nothing. He feels more comfortable among rocks.

Perhaps the television abstracts its events too much for him. He is more accustomed to being told directly by another person of a matter like death. "We had no radios or television, or anything but the conversation we made ourselves." When I ask him what he thinks of Eamon de Valera (whose constant dream it was to unite the North with the South), he replies, with a smile, "I don't know, because I never met him. What do *you* think of Dev?"

Then I ask him if he remembers Peig Sayers. "And why wouldn't I? Peig's family and our family was in and out of the same two houses." Peig would have been a much easier person for him to reach out and touch than "Dev," who never went to the Blaskets. Indeed, Micheál recalls, the young lads and girls of the island would often touch Peig, even embrace her, after she had told them a ghost story of an evening, the better to reassure themselves. Did they want to make sure, by touching, that her ghosts weren't real? But in a way, they were very real indeed, and Peig's stories about them probably would have held a greater immediacy for her listeners than an account of a sectarian killing on the *other* island. For in Peig's time, which is nearly our own, the Blasket was already approaching the realm of the spirit, losing its own, more palpable blood.

To some extent, Micheál Hurley carries this "Republic" around inside him still, although it is now rather like a solitude. "The mainland for the islandman is the hardest place ever to live," he says. That may help explain his bewilderment in the face of the Northern troubles, too; the whole of Ireland has been a strangeness to him, of which the North, divided or not, is only a part, just like the island of Inishtooskert is a part of the Blaskets, the northernmost part. Really, Micheál is from another island: another century. Which means that television and machineguns are still outlandish to him, "difficult pancakes" (as the late Flann O'Brien would have said). "'If ever I get to Ireland . . .' that's what the old people in the Blasket used to say," he observes.

The island is complete in his memory.

"We were like one big family," says Máire Kavanagh, another former islander. "In the wintertime, if any of the householders went out of flour or tea or sugar, or anything, they used to all share it. They were all united." She lives in Dunquin, moving there in 1947. She has a vivid recollection of the day, six years later, when what she calls "the island family" vanished. She could look right out of her window and see the boat, "the nobbie," bringing in the last of the islanders: "My aunt came in and I was crying. She said, 'They're coming, on the nobbie,' and I didn't answer her. So she said, 'What's wrong?' If I'd talk, I'd have burst out — I was trying to keep in the crying. But she saw it, and she said, 'You're crying for your mother and brothers coming in to the mainland. Your mother is old and you'd want her here now, and not to be thinking of her in the winter.' Well, I said, 'That's right, but what I am thinking — how will they ever close that door?' It was the little house we had on the island, where we were born and reared. When I think that the door is closed forever . . ."

The Blasket people had always kept their doors open.